Teaching Communication and Reading Skills in the Content Areas

by
Dorothy Grant Hennings
Kean College of New Jersey

Phi Delta Kappa, Bloomington, Indiana

Cover design by Nancy Rinehart

For
Uncle Howard
and
Aunt Irene

Acknowledgments

The author extends many thanks to those teachers who shared their teaching successes and failures and who supplied examples of work produced by children in their classes. Special thanks go to Janet Gould, Joanne Donahue, and Roberta Hastie for contributing lengthy pieces written by their classes and for charts compiled by their students. As always, the author extends thanks to George Hennings who supplied the encouragement that got this project off the ground and into production. The author especially appreciates the cooperation of Phi Delta Kappa's editor of Special Publications, Derek L. Burleson, who operates with an efficiency that other editors should emulate.

Illustration Credits

Facing page for Chapter 1
    Contributed by *Ann Marie Altavilla*
Page 25
    Contributed by *Susan George*
Facing page for Chapter 2
    Contributed by *Lisa Stellar*
Page 48
    Contributed by *Alison Cherris**
Facing page for Chapter 3
    Contributed by *Ari Globerman*
Page 77
    Contributed by *Kristen Wissel**

*Courtesy of Roberta Hastie, teacher,
Lincroft School, Lincroft, N.J.

Contents

v

Figures

Introduction

A key purpose of the language arts program is to help children and youth to master basic communication processes and those thinking processes associated with communication. Through the language arts students should grow in their ability to listen and speak, to read and write, and to use language to think. But students must read about something, talk about something, write about something, listen to ideas about something. This "something" can be content supplied by a literary selection or by a firsthand or vicarious experience; or—as this book emphasizes—it can be content from the natural and social sciences or from current events.

If students are to learn to communicate with one another about ideas and problems in the curriculum content areas, especially in science, social studies, and health, then it follows that instruction should be organized so that students acquire control over the facts, concepts, and generalizations of the subject areas; and control over skills related directly to those areas (e.g., map skills in the social studies). Instruction should also be organized to help children to communicate about content from the subject areas, specifically by gaining control over the skills of listening, speaking, reading, writing, and the thinking processes related to the content areas. This book is written for teachers who want to know how to incorporate language skill-building activity into subject-area teaching and learning.

This book has three major divisions: one on comprehension and study skills, a second on vocabulary development, and a third on writing skills. The reader will find overlap among the chapters, because there is really no way to separate reading, writing, listening, and speaking activities in teaching. Children listen, talk, and read in preparing to write; they listen as part of the discussion that typically follows reading and writing in the content areas. Talking and discussing permeate all learning; and listening and reading are necessary to comprehend subject matter content. For the same reason, the chapter on writing incorporates reading, listening, and speaking in an integrated language arts approach that blends instruction in communication processes with instruction in the facts, concepts, generalizations, and skills of various content areas.

This book provides practical teaching strategies that are based on research on how children learn to read and communicate. From such research the author synthesizes instructional strategies for the teacher who wishes to integrate communication skills with content study.

A final thrust of this book is involvement. Students need to be involved emotionally and intellectually if they are to learn. Therefore, numerous suggestions are offered for involving children and youth in communicating about content through talking, listening, writing, reading, observing, and doing. Viewed from this perspective, the communication processes are exciting ways of involving students actively and directly in learning content.

Dorothy Grant Hennings
Warren, New Jersey
June 1982

Differences

Colonist
hostile, annoyed
settling, protesting, fighting
farmers, freedom fighters; British, controller
uncaring, ruling, lawmaking
cruel, rich
King George III

1

Teaching Comprehension and Study Skills Across the Curriculum

Whatever you cannot understand, you cannot possess.

Johann Wolfgang von Goethe,
Maxims

Artwork and text contributed by
Ann Marie Altavilla

Teaching Comprehension and Study Skills Across the Curriculum

Students most often learn content through listening and reading. To learn the significant facts, concepts, and generalizations of a discipline is to listen and read for meaning. In oral communication the listener's task is to understand the message of the speaker, whether that message is delivered in a conversational setting that allows for immediate feedback or in a more formal lecture setting that may or may not allow the listener to respond. The same is true in reading. The reader's task is to go beneath the surface structure of letters and words to get at the meanings the writer intended.

Also, fundamental in learning content are what are generally termed study skills: the ability to locate material that bears upon a topic under investigation and the techniques for studying that material so as to comprehend it. Study skills, especially as they relate to reading, overlap in some respects with comprehension skills.

How does the teacher help young people build comprehension and study skills in the content areas? The pages that follow attempt to answer this question by suggesting ways to organize units of instruction that integrate language skills and content activity. In this chapter the author begins by identifying key comprehension and study skills that young people must acquire if they are to learn through listening and reading. Next, a generalized model for teaching comprehension and study skills in content areas is proposed, followed by specific instructional and learning strategies.

Comprehension and Study Skills to Be Taught

Comprehension skills that can be taught through unit study are of four types: factual, inferential, relational, and judgmental. These skills are common to both listening and reading for meaning. In addition, with listening, personal factors such as gestures, facial expressions, stance, and vocal intonations impinge on comprehension. With reading, the way material is laid out on the page can affect a student's ability to derive meaning.

Factual Comprehension

To comprehend at the factual level, a student must be able to grasp information in a reading passage or from what is stated directly by a speaker. In the case of listening, this means remembering the main ideas and significant details of a message heard, recording on paper a set of notes in which main ideas and details are clearly laid out, and acting upon information in the message, such as following directions. In the case of reading, it also means being able to locate needed information within the printed lines.

Comprehending main and subordinate ideas. When reading or listening to complex content, students cannot necessarily retain all the points raised, but should come away with the big ideas that are the essence of the message. In material from the natural and social sciences, the big ideas are often generalizations that explain how the world of nature works and how people function. Important details provide information about who, what, when, where, and under what conditions.

Taking notes. When oral messages or written passages are lengthy or complex, students cannot rely on memory alone in order to retain the main ideas and significant details. Therefore, they must acquire basic notetaking skills so that they can organize information in a way that is useful for them. Starting in grade three or four, students should be introduced to notetaking in order to develop skill in organizing information in a variety of formats as part of reading and listening. By the intermediate grades, young people typically are introduced to the conventions of formal outlining with main heads and subheads. In addition to formal outlining, students should also learn how to develop data retrieval charts, flow charts, maps, simple lists, and charts that outline who, what, when, where, under what conditions, why, and how. They should learn to vary their notetaking based on the purposes of their listening or reading, and on the kind of content they are handling.

Taking action on factual communication. When students organize information they hear or read into some logical scheme on paper, they are taking action on the information received. They are taking action on information when directions are given, such as in science, social studies, art, music, or physical education classes when the teacher orally outlines what students will do. For example, the science teacher may explain or

3

a laboratory guide sheet may describe how to manipulate a microscope. Whether the explanation is oral or written, clear comprehension is vital, because students who do not understand the dos and don'ts of microscope use can damage the slide or the microscope. The same is true with directions given in physical education classes. Failure to comprehend such directions can result in injury to students as well as to equipment.

Although some would claim that learning facts is less important than higher levels of thinking involved in inferential, relational, and judgmental comprehension, the first level of understanding is factual comprehension and it is basic. Unless students have the facts straight, they cannot render judgments about them, discover relationships among them, or act upon them. Paul Brandwein, in the Teacher's Edition of *Concepts in Science: Blue,* pg. T-9 (Harcourt Brace Jovanovich, 1980), makes this point clear, especially as it relates to scientific learning, when he states:

> Investigations, and the experiments they may include, come out of knowledge and not, as is often implied, a lack of knowledge. A scientist does not start with a problem; a scientist starts by *knowing something.* So does a teacher. So does a child.

In a similar vein, Robert Gagne, in *The Conditions of Learning,* 3rd ed. (Holt, Rinehart and Winston, 1977), writes:

> Knowing a set of strategies is not all that is required for thinking; it is not even a substantial part of what is needed. To be an effective problem solver, the individual must somehow have acquired masses of structurally organized knowledge. Such knowledge is made up of content principles . . .

Inferential Comprehension

To comprehend at the inferential level, students must be able to pick up meanings implied rather than stated directly by a speaker or writer. To do this requires that students be able to identify subtle clues. For example, a written passage or an oral message may not state directly the year or time of day when an event occurred, the age of the participants, the distances involved, or the precise location of an event. By reading or listening "between the lines," however, a person can figure out these details, as consideration of the following passage demonstrates:

> Abigail lay awake in her trundle bed. She could not sleep. She was thinking of tomorrow morning when the people of the settlement would gather to give thanks for the first harvest they had enjoyed in this new land.

4

In the days before, the men of the settlement had gone into the woods to shoot wild fowl and deer. The women had prepared cranberry relishes, corn, pumpkins, and the venison and wild turkeys for the feast that the settlers would share with some of the friendly Indians who lived nearby.

Abigail closed her eyes and imagined the good day to come. The last year had been hard. Often there was not enough food to eat. The first winter had been cold, and many of the settlers had become sick. But tomorrow would be different. She could hardly wait.

This passage does not identify the group of settlers as Pilgrims, the celebration as the first Thanksgiving, the time as early 1600s, the location as New England. Perceptive readers, who bring their prior knowledge to bear on the passage, get these points through inference. The same is true with implied meanings in an oral message. In either case, inferences can be judged correct or incorrect by referring to the content of the original message.

Readers and listeners can also make inferences about feelings or points of view contained within a message. A simple feeling inference about the passage above is that Abigail was excited about the coming feast day. In other instances, students may have to infer whether a speaker or writer is positive or negative on an issue or happy or unhappy about the events described. At times students must even infer the name of the individual about whom a speaker or writer is talking, especially in a sensitive situation where the writer or speaker does not want to come out and name names. But a speaker may drop subtle hints that perceptive listeners will pick up and thus know who the person in question is. Of all the content areas, the social studies provide the best context for helping young people build inferential comprehension skills.

Relational Comprehension

To comprehend at the relational level, students go beyond what is stated explicitly or implicitly. They must think in terms of why and how and then propose generalizations that are based on the points stated. In relational comprehension there are no right or wrong answers. Rather, students propose original statements of relationships, hypotheses, or predictions that appear to be consistent with given facts. The essence of relational comprehension is making the intellectual leaps that carry the thinker beyond given facts to propose relationships among those facts and to make predictions based upon them.

5

When presenting significant content from the subject areas, teachers should be alert for opportunities to help students see relationships. By doing this, students are engaging in truly creative reading and listening, because they are putting pieces together and discovering relationships for themselves. As students build their relational comprehension skills, they are functioning at a much higher intellectual level.

Judgmental Comprehension

To comprehend at the critical level, a student goes beyond the facts stated and renders value judgments on the message. Such judgments may focus on the factual content of the message, the assumptions underlying it, the opinions directly stated or the points of view implied, and even the style with which the message was presented. Of course, these judgments may also be influenced by the personal values of the student and go beyond the facts and opinions stated in a message.

When subject matter content deals with pressing social issues of past, present, or future, making judgments is no hypothetical exercise. Students are dealing with real issues that touch their own lives. Students are judging whether a particular act by a U.S. president was justifiable under the circumstances, whether specific revolutionary acts of a people were warranted, whether the position of country X or country Y was more acceptable, or whether a controversial research program should be continued. By the upper elementary grades, students are ready to examine the moral and ethical issues involved in these questions as part of the subject matter they are studying. When young people pursue these questions in their classes, they are developing critical comprehension skills and at the same time are learning content.

Nonverbal Comprehension Skills in Listening

In face-to-face situations, many aspects of a message may be communicated nonverbally. A raised eyebrow, a frown, a sudden movement of the arm may carry more meaning than the words spoken. To comprehend fully, students must be able to grasp these meanings. This is especially true if students are to go beyond factual meanings to consider implied meanings and to render value judgments. As listeners, students must be helped to understand:

1. Whether a speaker's verbal and nonverbal languages are sending compatible or conflicting messages;

6

2. How a speaker feels about a topic as indicated by his or her body language; and

3. How their own perceptions of nonverbal language (e.g., clothing, appearance, stance, mannerisms) affect their reaction to a message. Readers must handle some of these same features of communication when interpreting pictures in books and newspapers.

Study Skills Related to Reading

If young people are to become independent learners, they must be able to locate materials on a topic and be able to read and comprehend the material on their own. Specifically students must learn to:

1. Use the card catalog, indexes, and tables of contents to locate information on a topic;

2. Use boldface and italic headings as locational tools and as guides to the organization of a passage;

3. Use a variety of references including encyclopedias, dictionaries, almanacs, atlases, picture folios, and special indexes; and

4. Scan written material quickly to locate needed information and pass over material not related to the topic.

In addition, young people must develop their own approach to studying lengthy passages. They must learn how to get an overview before reading in detail, how to prepare for notetaking, and how to check their own comprehension after reading.

A unit study in any subject area is an ideal context for learning the skills of locating information and the skills of scanning. When using these skills while searching for information to share with others, youngsters see purpose in what they are doing. Then too, as part of a unit study, youngsters can practice these skills cooperatively with fellow students.

Summary

In this section we have discussed the four aspects of comprehension common to both listening and reading—factual, inferential, relational, and judgmental. In addition, the components of nonverbal language important to listening and study skills basic to independent reading have been outlined. Figure 1 presents these skills in the form of a checklist that teachers can use to diagnose children's skill levels and to develop programs in the content areas that include a comprehension and a study-skills dimension.

Figure 1   DIAGNOSTIC CHECKLIST OF
COMPREHENSION AND STUDY SKILLS

	Skill Levels			
The reader or listener is able to	*High*	*Average*	*Low*	*No Skill*
Factual Comprehension				
Distill main ideas from a message. Grasp significant details that support main ideas—who, what, when, where, and under what conditions.				
Organize ideas heard or read into a set of notes that meets the needs of the situation.				
Take action based on an oral or written communication, such as following a set of directions.				
Inferential Comprehension				
Grasp facts about time, distances, locations, people, and so forth, not stated explicitly but implied in the content.				
Infer the feelings and points of view of writer or speaker that are implied but not stated explicitly.				
Relational Comprehension				
Generalize based on given data. Predict outcomes not stated or implied.				
Hypothesize reasons not stated or implied.				

(continued on page 9)

8

Figure 1 (cont.)

Judgmental Comprehension

Render judgments about the content of a message, assumptions on which it is based, and opinions contained therein.

Render judgments about the style of a message.

Propose personal opinions and preferences in response to ideas stated; e.g., what he or she would do in the same or a similar situation.

Nonverbal Listening Comprehension

Interpret nonverbal signals in making inferences about implied meanings.

Use nonverbal signals in rendering judgments.

Study Skills in Reading

Use the card catalog, indexes, and tables of contents to locate information on a topic.

Use boldface and italic headings as locational tools.

Scan written passages quickly to locate needed information and to eliminate passages not relevant.

Use a variety of references.

Attack a written passage independently.

Student's Name: _____ Date: _____

Comments:

A Design for Teaching Comprehension and Study Skills in the Content Areas

Many teachers work on comprehension goals during regular reading periods using passages from graded basal readers. However, teachers tend to overlook that many of the same skills are basic to reading *and* listening comprehension, and that these skills can be blended while teaching content in classes other than reading. The following case study shows how this can be done in a sixth-grade social studies class.

Blending Reading and Listening Comprehension: A Case Study

Mr. Ortez's sixth-grade class is using the text, *The Human Adventure* (Addison-Wesley, 1976), as the jumping-off point for a unit study on civilizations down through the ages. At this point the class is dealing with the Renaissance and Age of Enlightenment in a module the text calls "Philosophers and Kings."

Gaining a Perspective on the Topic. To lay a foundation for future work with the topic, Mr. Ortez chose guided listening to the introduction to "Philosophers and Kings." Before beginning, Mr. Ortez asked his sixth graders to consider what the title "Philosophers and Kings" might mean and to tell what they knew about philosophers and kings. He then asked them to listen as he read them the introduction. When his students had listened to the section, Mr. Ortez guided them as they considered the major paragraphs. For a paragraph describing what the great philosophers of the 1600s and 1700s were writing, he asked, "What were the big ideas being voiced by the philosophers who lived then?" He asked the same question about successive paragraphs on John Locke, Montesquieu, and Rousseau. As the students responded, one of them wrote key points on the board under main headings the students themselves developed as they went along. These headings succinctly summed up the focus of each paragraph. They were:

I. What the philosophers of the 1600s and 1700s were saying
II. What John Locke wrote
III. What Montesquieu wrote
IV. What Rousseau wrote

When students had suggested points to list under these four headings, Mr. Ortez added three headings to the chalkboard.

    V. How these philosophers were similar
   VI. How these philosophers were different
  VII. How monarchs of the 1600s and 1700s would probably react to these ideas

Under Mr. Ortez's direction, the students opened their texts, reread the section silently to themselves, and then met in small groups to come up with points to list under each of these headings. Later they reconvened as a class to contribute their ideas to the chalkboard lists. Before erasing their notes from the chalkboard, one student made a copy on large chart paper for use later on.

Organizing for Comprehension. During the next social studies period, under Mr. Ortez's guidance, the class scanned the remaining 15 pages of the text on "Philosophers and Kings." They quickly looked through a subsection called "The Sun King" to identify him as Louis XIV of France; similarly they scanned sections called "The Double Eagle," "A Military State," "The Romanovs," and "In England" to identify the kings and queens and the periods and places where these monarchs ruled.

Based on this initial reading survey, the students organized a chart (see figure 2) to use in gathering notes about the royal houses described in their text.

Figure 2 A NOTETAKING GUIDE

Kings and Queens of the 1600s and 1700s
Name of king or queen: Name of royal house: Time frame: Place frame: What the monarch did: What the monarch believed or said: How what the monarch did related to what the philosophers were saying:

Having prepared for data collection, the students divided into five teams of four or five members. Each team was responsible for compiling a chart or a series of charts (if more than one member of a ruling house was described in the text) from reading the appropriate subsection of the text. Accordingly, there were teams on "The Sun King," "The Habsburgs," "The Kings of Prussia," "The Romanovs," and "The Kings and Queens of England." Besides gathering data from their text, the teams were to locate additional information on their topics through reading in related references. All information was to be placed on a display chart adhering as closely as possible to the ordering of topics cooperatively determined by the class.

Students worked in their teams for several days, going to the school media center when necessary to pick up needed references to bring back to the classroom. One team found and viewed a film related to the monarch for which it was responsible. Another located a relevant filmstrip. One student located books in the public library that the class could scan for information and placed them in the classroom reading corner. The charts grew in length and complexity as students went way beyond the material in their texts to ferret out data. As teams began to complete their charts, they met briefly with Mr. Ortez, who offered suggestions and discussed key points with them. Then they mounted the charts around the room so that the entire class could see them.

Analyzing Findings. With all the charts mounted, Mr. Ortez convened the class as a seminar. Members of each team first explained their charts to the class so that all would have some understanding of key findings. Then Mr. Ortez asked for comparisons and contrasts. He asked, "How was Louis XIV similar to the Habsburgs? to the Romanovs? to the monarchs of England? How was he unique?" When students had compared what the European monarchs were saying and doing, Mr. Ortez unrolled the chart the class had devised at the beginning of the unit that summarized the ideas of the philosophers of the period. He asked, "How do you think Rousseau would have felt about the policies of Louis XIV? How would John Locke have viewed Charles I of England? What would Montesquieu's probable reaction have been to the Kings of Prussia?" With such questions asked at this point, Mr. Ortez was getting his sixth graders to go beyond stated facts and to propose relationships. To get them to think judgmentally, he asked, "Under which monarch would you have preferred to live? Why?"

During the discussion, a recorder stood by the board and compiled a list of key points being made. Mr. Ortez stopped periodically for suggestions as to how best to organize the listening notes being written on the board. At this point, Mr. Ortez asked students to make a prediction. He asked, "Given the differences between the views of the monarchs and the philosophers, what could happen in Europe? Why? What factors support your prediction?" He also asked students to play with metaphorical relationships by suggesting, "I could call Europe under the Romanovs and the other monarchs a 'keg of dynamite.' Why? What else could we call Europe of that period? What about a car speeding out of control on a busy road? Why?" These questions were clearly relational, for they asked the students to go beyond stated facts to consider possible outcomes. They also laid the foundation for future study of the next unit in their text, "Revolution in America and France."

Designing Lesson Sequences

Mr. Ortez's lesson series suggests a sequence useful in teaching comprehension and study skills in the content areas. The sequence includes *perspective setting, organizing for reception, reception,* and *analysis.*

Perspective Setting. In learning content, students handle a lot of material that makes many points quite rapidly. In such situations, students need help in developing a mental framework for structuring the points and for distinguishing main and subordinate ideas as a basis for clarifying relationships. To build this framework readers will find it helpful to begin by studying carefully the introductory paragraphs of a reading selection to see if there are clues as to the overall direction the selection will take. Then, by rapidly scanning the main and subordinate headings, noting italicized words, and studying pictures and other visuals, a student has some understanding of the overall design of the section.

In listening situations, students can do much the same by attending to introductory remarks made by a speaker to identify any key themes to be developed in the presentation and to identify the structure or organization of the remarks to come. For example, if a speaker announces early on, "I am going to talk about four points," such a phrase gives the listeners a clue that they should be listening for those four points. To set the stage for purposeful listening, the teacher proposes a listening task: (e.g., "What problems were the people facing then that concerned the philosophers?").

Perspective setting techniques, such as those described above, should be used whenever students begin a major unit

13

involving a lot of reading material. As Mr. Ortez's introductory lesson suggests, textbook material can also be presented orally with the teacher reading it in a dramatic way. Students can begin to understand what is involved in really studying a written passage by reacting to passages as part of a cooperative listening experience. Also, if a unit introduction is oral, it helps slow readers to compensate for their lack of reading skill.

When a listening experience is used to set a perspective for what will follow, it provides an ideal opportunity to teach notetaking skills. As Mr. Ortez's lesson demonstrates, students can cooperatively develop a set of listening notes on the chalkboard in response to introductory material, which can then be converted into a chart for use as a reference throughout the unit.

Although research shows that the textbook usually serves as the major source of information in the content areas, teachers can start a unit by reading a selection from a trade book or a storybook that treats the period or problem that is the focus of unit study. Or they can show a film or filmstrip or share an audiotape. Whatever the approach, experienced teachers have found that it pays to guide students' listening or viewing activity by providing a perspective for assimilating what is to follow.

Organizing for Reception. The purpose of students taking notes as a response to listening and reading activities in the content areas is to help them organize points in a way that improves comprehension. Students need guided practice in organizing the information they are receiving. Initially, a teacher must guide the students in learning how to organize a set of notes.

No one format suffices for all notetaking situations, so students must be encouraged to think about what is the best way to record key points. In some cases, the data retrieval charts in chapter 3 on pages 67 and 83 are useful, especially when information comes from more than one source and will be used for writing summaries. In other cases, a list of key points, as in figure 2 on page 11, is more helpful, especially when several students are working on different aspects of a topic and need to compare their findings. In still other cases, notes can be visuals or pictures. Students may decide that the best way to sum up ideas on immigration patterns is with a map that uses arrows to show directions of migrations and labels to indicate the dates and the peoples involved. A rough sketch of an organism, a structure, or a piece of equipment might be more helpful in clarifying relationships; or a flow chart that lays out happenings, causes, and effects may be the best way to visualize big ideas.

14

Purposeful Reception. When assigning listening and reading activities, students will be more receptive if they can see a purpose. Purposeful reception is more likely to occur in a unit study because reading and listening serve as a means of data collection; and purpose is achieved if students know that data collected will help them see relationships among ideas about the topic under investigation. The primary task for the content-area teacher is how to make purposeful reception happen.

One way is to organize listening and reading so that each experience focuses on the broader topic or problem under discussion. This is in marked contrast to reading textual matter in a science, social studies, or health book paragraph by paragraph, and answering teacher questions on each discrete section.

A second way is to organize so that every student does not have to read every paragraph. In unit study, certain students can read specific sections that they will share later with others who have read different sections. Knowing that they will eventually share what they have learned gives purpose to their activity. This approach also means that there will be a blending of reading, listening, and speaking activity.

A third way to achieve purposeful reception is to use the textbook as a jumping-off point for gathering data, but then have students augment their findings by locating and reading related references or by viewing films and filmstrips. The textbook can provide an organizing framework for unit study, but all students need not read every word of the text. They can use the text as a base and search for and read references that supply related ideas and facts. In elementary classrooms, resources might include copies of other graded texts, encyclopedias, trade books, and storybooks.

Thinking About. As stated earlier, there are four levels of comprehension: factual, inferential, relational, and judgmental. At some point students must have opportunity to think about content in these four ways. The types of questions a teacher asks in large measure determine the cognitive operations students will use with the content they are studying. While it is important that teachers ask questions that get at who, what, when, where, and under what conditions to see if students grasp basic facts and ideas, they must ask questions that require students to show relationships, to make inferences, and to render judgments. Questions that encourage children to go beyond the facts include those that ask for:

1. Comparisons and contrasts: In what ways is this situation (problem, event, person, period, process) similar to that

one? How do these situations differ? What other situation is most like this one? Most different?

2. Groupings: What do these situations have in common that allows us to group or categorize them? What is the basis for our grouping? In what other ways can we organize facts and ideas? How can we lay out our data on paper to clarify similarities and differences?

3. Labels: What labels can we invent to apply to categories we have developed? What can we call this? What can we call that?

4. Explanations and generalizations: Why did (does) this happen? What are possible reasons? Is there a general statement that we can use to explain situations like this?

5. Preferences, opinions, and judgments: If you were given your choice of X, Y, and Z, which would you choose? Why? What do you think is the best course of action? Why? Of these two options, which is the more sensible? Why? Can you think of a better course of action?

6. Creative metaphors: To what can we compare this situation in a creative way? Why can we call this situation a keg of dynamite? a space ship? a flow? a cycle? a pendulum? a spiral? What else can we call it?

Dolores Durkin (1979) differentiates between teacher questions that assess children's ability to comprehend and questions that build comprehension skills. Her studies of classroom sessions in which students were involved in content learning indicate that few teachers actually build comprehension skills as part of unit study.

Not only must teachers ask questions that go beyond facts, they also must help students identify clues that clarify meanings. These clues may be semantic (relating to word meanings), syntactic (relating to sentence meanings), intonational (relating to changes in pitch, pause, or speed in oral communication), or pictorial. Thus teachers might ask students to make inferences about time relationships by asking, "What words give us a hint as to when this event occurred?" Or in making inferences about a character in a story or about a historical figure, the teacher might ask, "What information does this short clause give us that tells us what kind of person this is?" Or after children have listened to a recording of a dramatic presentation, the teacher might ask, "What do we know about the mood of the speaker from that long pause that we hear?" By asking such questions, teachers are not simply assessing children's comprehension, but are developing their comprehension skills by pinpointing words, sentences, sounds, and visual components of a message that give clues to meaning.

The more sophisticated levels of comprehension are not likely to occur until after students have acquired considerable background through listening or reading. Once students lay out factual data from their listening and reading in chart form, they have before them considerable information with which to identify similarities and differences, to categorize and label findings, to generalize, and to judge. When teachers ask higher level comprehension questions, students can then see the importance of sound data in any generalizations or judgments they make. They learn that they must have facts to back up their ideas.

Contexts for Developing Comprehension Skills Across the Curriculum

Comprehension skills can be taught in a variety of contexts in the content areas. But different kinds of materials require different approaches. In contrast to storybooks, content in textbooks is often complicated and may require several readings before it is fully comprehended. In addition to textbooks, there are other types of print materials available for unit study that lend themselves to teaching comprehension skills. They include:

1. Newspapers and magazines,
2. Children's classroom newspapers and magazines,
3. General references such as dictionaries, encyclopedias, atlases, and almanacs,
4. Informational books,
5. Biographies and autobiographies,
6. Historical fiction,
7. Collections of folktales and myths,
8. Poetry books.

There are many ways of incorporating these printed materials into unit study. A teacher can introduce a unit by reading a brief first-person account of a happening, a poem that touches on feelings relative to the topic, or even a definition of a key term from the dictionary. As an introduction to a unit, picture storybooks can make a contribution. For example, young children, beginning a study of social change, read and discuss a little book like *Changes, Changes* (Macmillan, 1971), by Pat Hutchins. Older children beginning a study of conflict can listen while their teacher shares a book like *Bang Bang You're Dead* (Harper and Row, 1969) by Louise Fitzhugh and Sandra Scoppettone. These same kinds of materials can be used at the end of a unit to reinforce learnings. When students use a vari-

17

ety of print materials, they learn to vary their reading and listening habits depending on the purpose of their study and on the kinds of materials.

Nonprint materials that young people can use to build their comprehension skills are as varied as the print sources. They include:

1. Films, filmstrips, and filmloops
2. Audio- and videotapes
3. TV and radio programs

Such materials are available for all curriculum areas and can be used to teach subject matter and comprehension skills at the same time. For example, one third-grade teacher introduced a health unit on basic food groups by showing a filmstrip and asking her pupils to listen to identify the major food groups necessary for good health. She then helped them scan their text to get an overview by studying the headings, diagrams, and pictures. The children also viewed an educational television program that discussed the importance of exercise. They then made data retrieval charts based on their viewing of the filmstrip and the television program and on their scanning of the text. Later they went to references for additional information they had identified as necessary to their investigation. The use of all these resources added interest to the unit and the children learned how to get facts and ideas through a variety of media.

With the advent of relatively inexpensive microcomputers, the schools have access to new learning tools. These computers, which combine visualizations and print, may be the "reference books" of the future. Students can use them to call up information available on either commercially prepared programs or on programs prepared by local media specialists and teachers. With this new tool, the notion of comprehension must be expanded to include computer literacy—the ability to operate a microcomputer in order to get needed information from it and to use the computer to create programs for others to use. The next decade will see great advances in the use of microcomputers in the school. Both teachers and students will need to acquire the skills of computer literacy.

Summary

This section has described a generalized model of teaching for comprehension in the subject areas. The model includes the components: *perspective setting, organization for reception, purposeful reception,* and *thinking about.* Figure 3 graphically shows the interrelationships among the components.

Figure 3   A MODEL OF CONTENT-AREA COMPREHENSION COMPONENTS

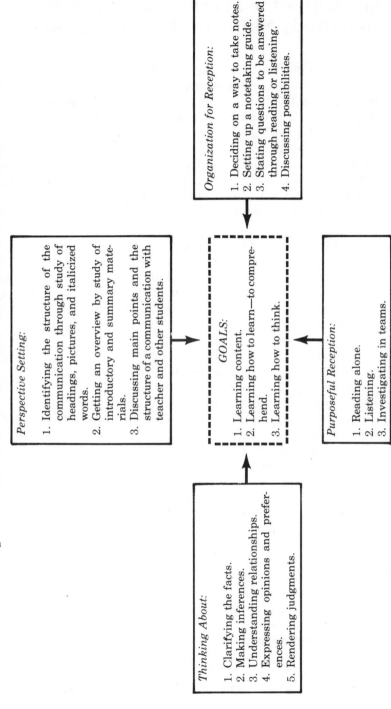

Organization for Reception:

1. Deciding on a way to take notes.
2. Setting up a notetaking guide.
3. Stating questions to be answered through reading or listening.
4. Discussing possibilities.

Perspective Setting:

1. Identifying the structure of the communication through study of headings, pictures, and italicized words.
2. Getting an overview by study of introductory and summary materials.
3. Discussing main points and the structure of a communication with teacher and other students.

GOALS:

1. Learning content.
2. Learning how to learn—to comprehend.
3. Learning how to think.

Purposeful Reception:

1. Reading alone.
2. Listening.
3. Investigating in teams.

Thinking About:

1. Clarifying the facts.
2. Making inferences.
3. Understanding relationships.
4. Expressing opinions and preferences.
5. Rendering judgments.

Strategies for Teaching Comprehension and Study Skills in the Content Areas

When reading and listening are integral parts of unit study in the content areas, children are building their comprehension and study skills through purposeful activity. They read and listen to find out, then go on to share their thoughts through writing and speaking. This is why unit study is an ideal framework for developing comprehension skills, because it blends all the language arts naturally as children learn content. In this section, we shall consider specific instructional strategies that lead to improved comprehension and that can be integrated easily into unit study.

Basic Listen/Read Strategies

The same skills are inherent in both listening and reading. Therefore, instructional strategies that integrate listening and reading are useful in building skills in both areas. These strategies can be classified as:

1. Listening and reading
2. Listening and rereading for detail
3. Reading along while listening along
4. Thinking about and feeling
5. Ordering, pairing, and categorizing

Listening and Reading. One way to structure lessons that build comprehension skills is to follow a listening activity with a reading activity. For example, one of the units in the third-grade Silver Burdett social studies text is transportation. The text, which includes pictures and short sentences that tell about the uses of cars, buses, trains, and planes, lends itself to an oral instructional approach. Using this material to build comprehension skills, the teacher might ask third graders to:

1. Study the introductory map and talk about forms of transportation shown on it;
2. Survey the pictures in the unit and decide what major topics will be covered;
3. Listen to the unit sentences as the teacher reads them, and under teacher guidance develop a chalkboard outline of main and subordinate topics;
4. Restudy the pictures to find more information to add to the outline; and
5. In small groups, write a single paragraph based on one

20

main topical heading of the outline.

The next unit in the third-grade Silver Burdett social studies program is on communication. With the experience gained in steps 1 through 5 above, with this unit the teacher may ask students to:

1. Survey the pictures to see if they can predict what the main topics of the unit will be and discuss their reactions. Then, record the main topics on the chalkboard.

2. Read to themselves the brief sentences of the selection to see if the topics they predicted to be the main ones are correct. Then, if changes or additions are needed, the students can edit their chalkboard outline.

3. Work in groups to add information under each of the topic headings by studying the textual material to get this information.

4. Add still more information to the outline by having the total class discuss points with the teacher.

5. Write a single paragraph summarizing the main points of their outline. This can be done in small writing groups or individually.

By structuring lessons so that students listen for a particular purpose (in this case, to identify main and subordinate points) and then read for the same purpose, the teacher is making the listening-reading connection.

Listening and Rereading. A second way to structure learning in the content areas to make the listening-reading connection is to ask youngsters to listen to a selection by the teacher and to identify the main topics. As the students suggest what the main topics are, they then record these on the chalkboard or on an overhead transparency. Then have the students open their books to the selection just read and ask them to reread it silently to see if they can identify subpoints that relate to the main topics already identified. If the main topics have been listed with space beneath, students can volunteer to insert subpoints into the developing outline. One of the advantages of this approach to learning in the content areas is that slower readers will hear unfamiliar vocabulary and new technical terms before encountering them in print. Also, during the discussion following the listening activity, students will likely use some of the new terms when they are developing their outline on the chalkboard or overhead projector. Thus vocabulary is being developed orally; students will have a meaning for these words before they read them.

Reading Along While Listening Along. Reading along while

21

listening along is another technique that helps the slower reader. However, to be effective the teacher's oral reading must be dynamic to hold listeners' attention. Avoid having a student read textual material aloud, paragraph by paragraph, if the student stumbles through the words and reads in a monotone. This is deadly to those listening and their attention will wander, or they may begin to read other sections of the text. Teachers must be sure that any oral sharing of material is performed in a dramatic way and that passages shared are kept short.

Thinking and Feeling About. As youngsters listen to or read material, they should be cognitively involved; this means getting the facts, making inferences, perceiving relationships, and rendering judgments. The kinds of questions the teacher poses determine in large measure how children approach their reading and listening. If the teacher asks only for information, children will tend to think in terms of getting the facts. However, if the teacher also requires children to make inferences, to generalize, and to render judgments, children will tend to look at facts from a different point of view.

Figure 4 is an example of a task sheet one teacher devised to develop comprehension in social studies content. Questions vary in their focus, starting with identifying basic information in the text and then moving on to some generalizing and decision making. Such task sheets are particularly useful as students work in groups after having read a selection individually. As they do the assignment, youngsters return to the material they previously read to find the needed information. In this way they learn that to understand a passage fully, they must often reread material, especially when the material is complex.

Ordering, Pairing, and Categorizing. When teaching content that deals with a series of events or steps, asking students to order those events or steps encourages them to think in terms of logical or chronological sequences. Once students have listened to or read a passage that involves a sequence or steps, give them a set of cards, each of which contains one item in the sequence, and ask the students to put them in order and explain the reasons for the sequence they have made. Or students can be asked to call out the events within sequences while the teacher or a student records them on a board or chart. Then, working on their own or in teams, the students can put events into a chronological or logical order. In much the same way, students can make judgments about the relative importance or significance of acts or events by ordering or ranking those acts or

Figure 4 A TASK SHEET THAT CHECKS FACTUAL, INFERENTIAL,
RELATIONAL, AND JUDGMENTAL COMPREHENSION*

Cities in Canada

Directions: Read "Cities in Canada" found on pages 277-282 of *Man and
Society*. Then answer the questions on this sheet.

1. Name the six largest Canadian cities and tell for what each is best known.
   (This is a factual question—the answer is stated explicitly in the text.)

The City   **What It Is Known For**

A.
B.
C.
D.
E.
F.

2. What crops are grown in Canada? What industries does Canada have? (This
   is an inferential question—the answer can be inferred from goods shipped
   to and from cities.)

The Crops   **The Industries**

3. Why is Montreal the largest and most important commercial city in Canada?
   (This is a relationship question—the reader must consider geographic factors, transportation facilities, past history, and sociological factors.)

4. The book calls Hamilton the Pittsburgh of Canada and Windsor the Detroit
   of Canada. Match a city in the United States with each of the six Canadian
   cities. Give one reason for each of your choices. Then decide in which one
   of the six Canadian cities you would most like to live and give your reason.
   (This is a relationship and judgmental activity—the reader must consider
   numbers of interrelated factors, make a decision, and support it with reasons.)

The Canadian City   **The United States City**   **Your Reason**

A.
B.
C.
D.
E.
F.

The City Where You Might Want to Live: _____   Your Reasons:

---

*from Hennings, Hennings, and Banich. *Today's Elementary Social Studies*,
p. 330. Copyright © 1980 Rand McNally Publishing Company. Reprinted by
permission of Houghton Mifflin Company.

events. When there is a difference of opinion, the students may have to take a vote or continue their discussion until they reach a consensus.

Students who have read or listened to content material that deals with cause-and-effect relationships can use cards to pair causes with effects; for example, they can pair terms with definitions, events with dates, and people with events or dates. They can also group items together that share a relationship. This last activity works well when students collect lots of facts and record them in random fashion on the chalkboard; then working together they categorize those that share a common feature.

In the approach described above, the teacher can initially prepare the cards that students order, pair, or group. But once students have had practice in this kind of activity, they can individually or in groups create similar cards and ask fellow students to match cards to show relationships.

Following is an instructional sequence that requires students to make judgments by ranking the importance of acts done by historical figures:

1. Students listen as the teacher reads a short biographical selection about a historical figure.

2. Students identify the specific acts performed by the historical figure, and a scribe records these acts on the board.

3. The teacher leads students in a discussion of the importance of these acts as they relate, for example, to the development of the nation. Students rank the acts from the most important to the least important.

4. Students then select a biography of a well-known historical figure to read independently. As they read, they keep a list of acts performed by the person in question.

5. In groups, students share key acts about their historical person. The group cooperatively decides how to rank the acts.

6. Later, the total class convenes as a seminar and decides on the ranking of all the historical figures discussed from the most important to least important. Through the discussion and debate involved in the ranking, students are having their content learning reinforced and are learning how to make judgments.

Basic Listen/Read/Write Strategies

If children are to think about the ideas they encounter through their listening and reading, they must do something with those

The Five Acts

Stamp Act	1 7 6 5	The colonists sometimes tarred and feathered the tax collectors.
Quartering Act	1 7 6 5	The Bostonians insulted the soldiers and threw rocks and snowballs.
Townsend Act	1 7 6 7	Used boycott peaceful resistance.
Tea Act	1 7 7 3	Colonists dressed up as Indians and threw the tea into the harbor
Intolerable Acts	1 7 7 4	Used boycott peaceful resistance.
by Susan George	4/21/82	
Information from: People in the Americas, Soc. Stu.		

Example of student notetaking

ideas. One form of "doing" is writing. Writing as a response to reading or listening might be simply notetaking or, at more advanced levels, compositions or poems.

Notetaking. Although children should probably learn the conventions of formal outlining, there is clearly no one way of notetaking. Notetaking must be adapted to the kind of material being studied. Making a list of key points is perhaps the easiest form of notetaking. Students can make such a list periodically during a discussion when the teacher asks, "What are the key points we have been making?" After students have had a number of opportunities to make such a list under the teacher's guidance, they can do it independently with the teacher moving about the class rendering assistance when needed. This same approach can be used to make summary-type notes after students have read a selection in their text.

Another form of notetaking can be guided by teacher-posed questions. By using question headings on a chart or chalkboard, the teacher can guide youngsters' thinking about a selection. What or whom is this passage about? When did or when will this happen? Where will or where has this happened? Such questions of the who, what, where, when, why, and how variety help children organize the content they are studying. These same questions can be used on a reading/listening individual work sheet that children use at their desks.

The type of listening/reading guides will vary depending on the content. Guides can be in the form of maps, flow charts, timelines, diagrams, and tables as well as in a question form. At first, the teacher may have to suggest the format for taking notes. Later, as youngsters become accustomed to looking at headings, pictures, and introductory material before reading a selection, they can cooperatively devise forms for notetaking, that are appropriate to the content being covered.

Composing. Writing activities are a natural outgrowth of listening and reading associated with unit study. For example, students can write letters to get information on a topic they have read about. Teaching the skills of letter writing has a real purpose in such situations. Other writing activities that can result from reading and listening associated with unit study include:

1. Odysseys: hypothetical trips through a state, country, or area being investigated.

2. Travel brochures: material advertising the virtues of a state, country, or area.

3. Illustrated glossaries: definitions accompanied by illustrative sketches.

4. Biographical sketches: descriptions of key events in a person's life.

5. First person accounts: mock diaries in which the writer pretends he or she is somebody else and writes from that point of view.

6. Editorials: paragraphs that express a point of view on an issue.

7. Plays: short dramatizations about a topic or event in unit study.

8. Poems: expressions of feelings about a topic using meter, rhyme, free verse, haiku and other poetic forms.

Reading and listening take on real purpose when students are expected to gather information for their own writing. By having in mind specific questions, students can develop a listening/reading guide, which becomes an outline to use in structuring ideas for writing.

Basic Listen/Read/Speak Strategies

The instructional strategies described so far involve children in talking out ideas. However, there are other forms of oral activities that develop comprehension as children begin to handle more complex content. These forms can be characterized as presentational rather than conversational.

Oral Interpretation and Dramatization. When content material has an especially dramatic quality, using oral interpretation becomes one way of checking for comprehension. An exciting passage from a biography or autobiography, a poem, or even an editorial can be used for oral interpretation if students prepare for it. By preparing, the student has to rehearse the passage and decide where to pause, to place emphasis, to change pitch and tone in order to communicate the meaning of that passage to others. Another form of oral interpretation is dramatization. When content material is in a conversational format, students can assume the roles of those speaking within the passage, with one student serving as narrator. Using this approach adds interest to the study and gives the teacher an opportunity to judge whether students can interpret the phrasing and punctuation patterns of a selection, for to understand a passage fully, a reader must be able to interpret the meanings communicated by punctuation marks and must be able to read not individual words but blocks of words or phrases that serve as units of communication.

SQ3R Approach to Reading Comprehension

One approach long advocated by reading specialists to help students get meaning from written passages is called SQ3R, which stands for Survey, Question, Read, Recite, Review. Using SQ3R, students begin by surveying the material by checking headings, pictures, and introductory and summary sections as was described earlier. Based on their initial surveys, readers formulate a series of questions to be answered while reading the material. This step as an individual study plan is comparable to what was previously termed *preparation for reception,* because the questions thus formulated essentially serve as a reading guide. Having prepared for reception, students read to answer the questions, making notes as they progress through the selection. Next, readers recite or answer the questions to themselves. The recitation step is critical in understanding complex content, because through it readers have the opportunity to verbalize that content, to put it in their own words. Reciting to one's self serves not only as a reinforcement but as a self-test. Having recited, students review the material to pick up points missed on the first go-round.

At some point during unit study, students should have guided practice with the SQ3R approach. Teacher and students can work through a passage several times orally, using the survey, question, recite, and review steps until all know what the passage is about. Later, students can handle comparable passages in the same way on their own. Later still, students can work cooperatively in teams and carry out the recite step orally and then return to their texts to review the material that they missed or did not understand.

The strategies described above are a far cry from the practice of reading from a text, sometimes orally paragraph by paragraph in round-robin style, and responding to questions posed by the teacher or to those given at the end of a chapter. Clearly, such a practice is limiting and unchallenging. Children are not being given systematic instruction in reading comprehension skills; and little attention is being given to listening skills. This chapter has detailed numerous strategies that make skill development relative to listening and reading an integral part of unit study. Using these strategies, teachers can design innovative units in the content areas that enable children to grow in comprehension skills as they are learning content.

Summary

Four major generalizations from this chapter are summarized below:

1. Many of the skills fundamental to comprehending written material are also fundamental to comprehending an oral message. Accordingly, activities to build reading comprehension skills should be blended with activities to build listening comprehension skills.

2. Basic listening/reading comprehension skills include the ability to get the facts (factual comprehension), the ability to make inferences based on material read or heard (inferential comprehension), the ability to see relationships based on material read or heard (relational comprehension), and the ability to render sound judgments based on material read or heard (judgmental comprehension). These skills should be a part of study in the content areas.

3. As students are building their listening and reading comprehension skills, they should be involved in lots of talking and writing activity, which are natural outgrowths of listening and reading.

4. When teachers organize instruction in the content areas into unit studies, students will acquire basic comprehension skills at the same time they are learning content.

Related References

Durkin, Delores. "What Classroom Observations Reveal About Reading Comprehension Instruction." *Reading Research Quarterly* 14 (1978-1979): 481-533.

_____ . "What Is the Value of the New Interest in Reading Comprehension?" *Language Arts* 58 (1981): 23-43.

Estes, Thomas, and Vaughan, Joseph. *Reading and Learning in the Content Area Classroom.* Boston: Allyn and Bacon, 1978.

Gerhard, Christian. *Making Sense: Reading Comprehension Improved Through Comprehension.* Newark, Del.: International Reading Assn., 1975.

Guthrie, John, ed. *Cognition, Curriculum, and Comprehension.* Newark, Del.: International Reading Assn., 1977.

_____ . "The 1970s Comprehension Research." *Reading Teacher* 33 (April 1980): 880-882.

Hennings, Dorothy. *Russell and Russell's Listening Aids Through the Grades.* rev. ed. New York: Teacher's College Press, 1979.

Henry, George. *Teaching Reading as Concept Development: Emphasis on Affective Thinking.* Newark, Del.: International Reading Assn., 1974.

Lundsteen, Sara. *Listening: Its Impact at All Levels on Reading and the Other Language Arts.* Urbana, Ill.: National Council of Teachers of English, 1979.

Page, William, and Pinnell, Gay. *Teaching Reading Comprehension: Theory and Practice.* Urbana, Ill.: National Council of Teachers of English, 1979.

Pearson, P. David, and Johnson, Dale. *Teaching Reading Vocabulary and Teaching Reading Comprehension.* New York: Holt, Rinehart and Winston, 1978.

Schulwitz, Bonnie, ed. *Teachers, Tangibles, Techniques: Comprehension of Content in Reading.* Newark, Del.: International Reading Assn., 1975.

Smith, Frank. *Comprehension and Learning.* New York: Holt, Rinehart and Winston, 1975.

Stauffer, Russell, and Cramer, Ronald. *Teaching Critical Reading at the Primary Level.* Newark, Del.: International Reading Assn., 1968.

Thomas, Ellen, and Robinson, Alan. *Improving Reading in Every Class: A Sourcebook for Teachers.* 2nd ed. Boston: Allyn and Bacon, 1977.

Wolvin, Andrew, and Coakley, Carolyn. *Listening Instruction.* Urbana, Ill.: National Council of Teachers of English, 1979.

Lisa Stellar

① boycott -
   v.
SENTENCE: A man with a big belly boycotted some goods.

② boycott -
   n.
SENTENCE: The boycott really worked.

No tea being unloaded

Vocabulary Development
Across the Curriculum

2

Vocabulary Development Across the Curriculum

Words are what hold society together.

Stuart Chase
Power of Words

Artwork and text contributed by
Lisa Stellar

Vocabulary Development
Across the Curriculum

Every discipline has its technical vocabulary. To describe and explain phenomena, biologists use such terms as *metamorphosis, genes, capillaries,* and *enzymes;* economists' vocabularies include *balance of payments, distribution of labor, inflation,* and *recession;* sociologists speak of *status, sanctions, role,* and *group;* chemists talk of *ions, molecular forces, molar solutions,* and *balanced equations.* To study a discipline is not only to understand the basic facts and the big organizing ideas of the field, it is also to learn the terminology of that discipline. Accordingly, subject-matter teachers must structure lessons to develop and refine students' word power as it relates to the subject being taught.

This chapter deals with the development of vocabulary skills. It begins by defining word skills important in subject-matter learning. It then describes a classroom situation in which vocabulary development is integrated into content learning and presents a model for teaching for word power. The final section of the chapter sets forth strategies for achieving vocabulary growth.

Vocabulary Development
in the Content Areas

Four objectives of vocabulary development in the content areas are:

1. Students should acquire a wide repertoire of words that are part of everyday usage and provide a base of common language meanings.

2. Students should understand and use technical words in reading, listening, talking, and writing that are commonly used by specialists in a field.

3. Students should be able to see relationships among words and to analyze the internal structure of words to figure out meanings of technical terms.

4. Students should be able to use the dictionary for figuring out word meanings, pronunciation, and normal usage patterns.

Building Common Language Meanings

Especially in content areas in the elementary grades, students must learn the meaning of commonly used words associated with that content. In reading or listening, youngsters may encounter a common word that holds no meaning for them. For example, the sentence: "The two countries jockeyed for power as the world watched to see which would better the other," makes little sense to a reader who does not have a clear idea of the word *jockey,* or knows the word only in the context of horse racing. In their studies, youngsters will meet many words that are commonly used in everyday interaction but also have a specialized meaning within a discipline. The word *urban,* for example, is part of our general vocabulary, but the social scientist uses it in a special context when referring to geographical areas with certain characteristics.

Using such words as *jockeyed* and *urban* does not result from memorized definitions. Rather, growth in functional vocabulary occurs gradually through the processes of assimilation and accommodation, through which youngsters attach meanings to words by hearing, reading, and trying them out, and by refining those meanings by using them in a variety of contexts. Piaget calls the process through which children attach meanings to words "assimilation" and the process through which they refine those meanings "accommodation."

How these processes operate is made clear by observing the language development of children. If a child is given a big beach ball and is asked, "Do you want to play with this ball?" the child may respond, "Play the ball," as he takes it and bounces it back to the parent. Later, the child may bring the beach ball to the parent and say, "Play the ball." The parent, expanding the child's remarks, may reply, "Do you want to play with the ball?" In the process the child hears the word again and comes to assimilate it into his word pool.

Later still, the child plays with a tennis ball and a small rubber ball. When the parent also calls each of these "a ball," the child enlarges his concept of ball to include these variations.

At some later time, that same child may see a honeydew melon and say, "Ball. Play the ball." At that point, the parent may respond, "That's a melon, not a ball." The alert parent may even encourage the child to touch and taste the melon so that he begins to build meanings relative to the term *melon* while refining, or accommodating, meanings associated with the word *ball.* Accommodation results from encounters that do not fit into the child's previous conceptual scheme; i.e., all round objects are not called balls. The process of assimilation and accommodation of common language meanings must be part of content-area study.

As students encounter a commonly used term in listening or reading, they may need to stop to clarify meanings. For example, the teacher may take a set of pictures that includes a tree, bluebird, rose, elephant, snail, snake, pine cone, and grass, and ask, "How can we categorize these things?" If the response is blank expressions, the teacher stops to clarify, "By categorize, I mean to put similar objects together in a group and other kinds of objects together in another group. Here is an orange. Is it more like the rose or the elephant? Why? Which other objects are like the orange and the tree?" As students name other forms of plant matter, the teacher writes *Category I: Plant Matter* and lists the forms of plant matter beneath that label. As students identify a second category—animal matter—the teacher writes *Category II: Animal Matter* and lists the forms of animal matter. Throughout the discussion the teacher continues to use the terms *category* and *categorize,* asking, "Into which of our two categories does a human being belong? How should we categorize a deer? a tulip? a squash?" On successive days, as students go on to categorize animals into subgroups such as mammals, fish, and reptiles, and plants into subgroups such as fruits and vegetables, the teacher and the students continue to use *category* and *categorize* as part of their speaking vocabulary. In this way, they are building common language meanings as they acquire understanding of basic content.

Building Technical Language Meanings

In learning subject matter students must be able to comprehend technical words met during listening and reading and be able to use those words in talking and writing. To use technical vocabulary requires that the student first have a conceptual understanding of terms. One of the best ways to build this conceptual understanding is by using specific examples to which children can attach terms or labels. By using the specific examples students learn how a particular term is applied and gradually build a network of meanings related to that term.

As students inductively learn concepts by starting with specific examples and then building generalizations based on these examples (assimilation), they begin to encounter additional examples to which they can apply the generalization. Then they can begin to communicate the concept by using the appropriate term in their speaking and writing. With further

34

application, students refine their understanding of the way a particular word is used. This is the accommodation phase of concept development.

As students assimilate the meanings associated with a technical term, they should also learn to pronounce and spell it. The instructional sequence should provide for both clear pronunciation and writing of technical terms. Vocabulary building requires an integration of listening, speaking, reading, and writing.

Figuring Out Word Meanings

Students can figure out the meaning of a new word by using a combination of word analysis strategies: 1) structural analysis, 2) word-relationship analysis, and 3) contextual analysis.

Structural Analysis. By using the structural elements of words, such as prefixes, suffixes, and word roots, students can learn to figure out the meaning of many words. For example, a common prefix and a common suffix make up the word *geology.* If students know from previous contact with *geography* that *geo* means earth and from previous contact with *biology* that *ology* means study of, they can easily decode the meaning of *geology.* If students know how the addition of a particular suffix affects the way in which a word functions in a sentence, they may be able to understand the word more readily. Such suffixes as *-ism, -tion, -ity, -ist, -ment, -ology, -er, -ee,* make words that function as nouns. The suffixes *-ize, -ate,* and *-ify* make words that function as verbs. The suffixes *-ous, -ive, -able, -ful,* and *-y* make words that function as adjectives. In the same way, the ability to see component words within compound words helps in figuring out word meaning.

Word-relationships Analysis. Closely related to the ability to analyze the structure of words is the ability to see relationships among words that are derived from the same roots. For example, the words derived from the Latin *communicare,* meaning to share, include *communicate, communication, commune, communicable, communicant;* also *community, communism, communist,* and *communize* as well as the distinctive *communique.* Students who meet the word *communique* for the first time in social studies will master its meaning quickly if they relate it to the familiar word *communicate.* Likewise, students who meet *communism, communist,* and *communize* may grasp the meanings of these words if they relate to the word *community.* An instructional design that has vocabulary development as one of its goals must help children make these kinds of word connections.

Contextual Analysis. As children listen and read, they can learn to figure out the meaning of a word from the context in which the word is used. Contextual clues include:

1. A definition of the new term built right into the context, as in the sentence, "Molecules, the tiny particles that are the building blocks of matter, are farther apart in gases than in liquids." Students must be alert for such definitions, which are essentially word equations.

2. A full description of an object being introduced for the first time. Thus in a passage about a blast furnace, students may find a brief definition or word equation, followed by paragraphs of description.

3. Pictures, diagrams, flow charts, or schematics. Science texts are filled with labeled diagrams that clarify terms used in the text. A good reader moves from visuals to verbal explanations and from verbal explanations to visuals in an attempt to figure out the exact meaning of a new term.

4. Use of the new term juxtaposed with a clarifying synonym. For example, in No. 1 above, the more common synonym *particle* is juxtaposed with *molecule* and helps to clarify the technical term.

5. Use of an antonym juxtaposed with the new term. If, for example, the word *immense* is used to describe a blast furnace and is contrasted with the word *small* used to describe an ordinary oven, then students will have a good clue to the meaning of the word *immense.*

Building Dictionary Use Skills

No matter what skills students have for figuring the meaning of words, some words may defy analysis. Here is where good dictionary use skills become important. Such skills include the ability to: a) locate a word through use of alphabetical order and guide words, b) pronounce the word based on the phonetic spelling provided, c) interpret which dictionary definition is appropriate for how the word is used in a sentence, and d) crosscheck from one dictionary entry to another. That last skill is important when an unfamiliar word appears in the definition, and the students must check in another part of the dictionary in order to get the meaning of the original word.

Vocabulary growth should be an ongoing component of content-area study. Figure 5 provides a checklist of vocabulary skills that can be used as a diagnostic tool or as a design for instructional strategies for vocabulary growth.

Figure 5   VOCABULARY SKILLS CHECKLIST

The student is able to:	Above Average for Grade Level	Average for Grade Level	Below Average for Grade Level
I. Word usage skills			
A. Interpret the meanings of commonly used words when encountering them in reading and listening.			
B. Interpret the meanings of technical terms when encountering them in technical reading and listening.			
C. Use common words to express relationships in speaking and writing; pronounce and spell words in functional speaking and writing vocabularies.			
D. Use technical words to express relationships in speaking and writing about phenomena in the natural, social, and symbolic worlds; pronounce and spell technical vocabulary.			
II. Word analysis skills			
A. Use common prefixes and suffixes in figuring out word meanings.			
B. Use the meaning of a known root in figuring out a new word.			
C. Dissect compound words to figure out the meaning of new words.			
D. Associate one word with others derived from a common root.			
E. Derive definitions from context in which words are used.			
F. Interpret extended descriptions related to key terminology in order to figure out meanings.			

(continued on page 38)

Figure 5 (cont.)			
G. Interpret pictures, charts, diagrams, etc. that give a clue to word meanings.			
H. Utilize synonyms and antonyms as clues to word meaning.			
III. Dictionary use skills			
A. Locate a word through use of alphabetical order and guide words.			
B. Pronounce a word based on phonetic spelling.			
C. Interpret the dictionary definition by how the word tends to function in a sentence.			
D. Crosscheck dictionary entries.			

Student's Name: _____ Date: _____

Comments: _____

A useful practice at the beginning of a unit is to list the key technical terms to be learned. These become a checklist for the teacher to assess whether a student can interpret these words in listening and reading and can use them in speaking and writing. Figure 6 provides a format for assessing a student's vocabulary growth in a particular content unit.

Figure 6　　VOCABULARY CHECKLIST FOR A CONTENT UNIT

List of key words in unit	*The student is able to use these words in*			
	listening	*speaking*	*reading*	*writing*

A Design for Teaching Vocabulary in the Content Areas

How does the teacher of science, social studies, health, or even mathematics structure a learning sequence so that students develop vocabulary to express themselves in those fields and so that they are able to interpret word meanings when they encounter new terminology in their listening and reading? In this section we shall present a case study of a seventh-grade science lesson in which vocabulary development is an integral part. Generalizing from this case study, we shall propose a design for teaching vocabulary in the content areas and suggest several instructional strategies for building vocabulary.

Vocabulary Growth in Content Learning: A Case Study

Ms. Stone's introduction to the science lesson on the properties of matter was a bit unusual. She handed each youngster a piece of masking tape. When all students had a piece of tape, Ms. Stone asked them to stick it on their forearms. She did the same with hers and asked, "Who can tell me what is happening?"

One student replied, "The tape is sticking to my skin."

"Let's be more precise," Ms. Stone urged, "Yesterday what did we say we called the particles that make up all matter?" When one student responded, "molecules," she said, "Who can now explain what is happening with the tape using the word *molecules*?"

Another student answered, "The molecules of the tape are sticking to the molecules of the skin."

At this point, Ms. Stone held up another kind of tape and asked, "What's this?" When a girl answered, "adhesive tape," Ms. Stone asked her to write the word *adhesive* on the board by breaking it into syllables. She then stuck the piece of adhesive tape on the board and asked the students to explain what was happening, again using the word *molecules* in their answer.

A student explained, "The molecules of tape are sticking to the molecules of board."

"Good," said Ms. Stone, "but scientists use a word that means 'to stick' in talking of this phenomenon, a word that begins just like our word *adhesive*. Can somebody think of that word?"

One youngster got the point and suggested *adhering*. Ms. Stone asked him to use it in a sentence that explained how the tape stuck to the board and asked another youngster to write the word *adhere* on the board. Looking at *adhere,* students talked about why the final *e* was dropped in forming *adhering.*

Next Ms. Stone introduced the word *adhesion* and asked students to guess its meaning based on the words they already knew. As she wrote the word on the board, she discussed how the suffix *-sion* changed the function of the word to a noun.

Having developed some of the basic vocabulary needed to describe the adhesive property of matter, Ms. Stone next set up a situation in which students could use their newly acquired vocabulary. She dipped a glass tube into a beaker of colored water, put her finger on the end of the tube, and asked children to describe the appearance of the surface of the water in the tube. Students used their hands to show the downward curve of the liquid, and one student sketched a diagram on the board. Ms. Stone drew the students' attention to the contact point between water and glass tubing, "What can we say is happening here?"

Students responded by talking in terms of water molecules adhering to glass molecules and of this being another example of adhesion. In each case, they explained what was happening using the terms *molecules, adhering, adhesion,* and *adhesive* in their descriptions.

At this point, Ms. Stone distributed 3 × 5 cards to the students and asked them to print the key technical term of the lesson, *adhesion,* showing its syllable pattern. She then asked, "What part of speech is *adhesion?*" Students recorded *noun* after the word on their Technical Vocabulary Cards. Cooperatively the youngsters put together a definition of the term and recorded it on their cards. Then they added associated words—*adhere, adhering, adhesive, adhered.*

For the next day's science lesson Ms. Stone poured colored water into a tumbler so that the water level could be seen over the rim of the glass. Then carefully she dropped in first one penny, then another, and still another. Although the glass seemed to be full before dropping in the coins, the water did not spill over. As the students discussed why the water did not spill over, they finally came up with the possibility of a force between water molecules that held the water together. "Could we call this force *adhesion?*" Ms. Stone asked. The youngsters decided no, because different kinds of molecules were not involved here, just water molecules. "Put a different prefix on adhesion and you will have the word that describes this force," suggested Ms. Stone. Students were soon talking of the cohesive force between water molecules, of cohesion, and of mole-

40

cules cohering. They used these terms to talk about several other demonstrations Ms. Stone did, such as floating razor blades on the water surface and using an eye dropper to make drops of water on a flat surface.

Throughout their doing and talking session, students came forward to record technical words on the board, divide them into syllables and check difficult spellings. At the end of the session, students prepared another Technical Vocabulary Card on which they recorded the main word, *cohesion,* with its definition, part of speech, and related words. They placed this card in alphabetical order in their science vocabulary box.

Only after students had done experiments and discussed the basic concepts relative to adhesion and cohesion over a period of three days, did Ms. Stone ask them to read the section in their texts that applied. By then their reading was an easy task, for they already knew the key vocabulary terms and had developed a rudimentary understanding of the concept.

After reading their texts, students performed other experiments explained in their texts and discussed other situations in which the concepts of adhesion and cohesion could be used to explain what was happening. Then Ms. Stone asked them to write, not individually but as a total class activity, because she wanted to teach writing skills, particularly how to use such words or phrases as *because* and *as a result* to communicate cause-and-effect relationships. Organizing the class as a teacher-guided writing group, she began by asking the students to think of a sentence they could use to introduce a paragraph about cohesion that would explain this phenomenon to other students. The class agreed that such a paragraph should begin with a definition of cohesion. Working from the vocabulary cards they had developed during the previous lesson, the students talked out possible ways of phrasing a beginning sentence or a topic sentence. Then, guided by Ms. Stone's request that they include sentences that supported what they had investigated during the previous lesson, the students offered sentences describing the pennies, razor blades, and droplets. Their paragraph, drafted cooperatively and recorded on the board, was as follows:

COHESION

Cohesion is the process by which molecules of the same kind of matter are attracted to one another. Pennies dropped into a full glass of water did not make the water flow over. Razor blades floated on the surface of the water. Droplets are round.

41

Next, Ms. Stone asked the seventh graders to study their paragraph, especially the beginning of sentence two, to decide what should be added to show the relationship between sentence one and two. Students rather quickly got the point and noted the need for an introductory phrase such as "Because of this force." Students also suggested that this same phrase belonged at the beginning of sentence three. Ms. Stone asked, "Rather than repeating the same phrase, what could we do with sentences two and three?" Students suggested combining sentences two and three to show that the same reason applied. They introduced the last sentence with the word "also" and ended it with the words "as a result of cohesion."

After the students had edited their paragraph to reflect logical relationships among ideas, Ms. Stone focused their attention on a verb tense problem by circling the first sentence. "Look here," said Ms. Stone, "and then check verb tenses throughout the paragraph." One student saw the problem of changing tenses and made the corrections at the board. The paragraph now read:

COHESION

Cohesion is the process by which molecules of the same kind of matter are attracted to one another. Because of this attraction between water molecules, pennies dropped into a full glass of water do not make the water overflow, and razor blades float on the surface of the water. Also droplets are round as a result of cohesion.

The next day, the class formed into three-person writing teams to compose and edit short explanatory paragraphs on adhesion. They used the structure of the cohesion paragraph as a model, starting with a definition and then giving examples that occurred as a result of that force.

To follow up the vocabulary work in science, Ms. Stone read some sentences to the class, leaving out key words to see if the class could suggest what words had been deleted. Sentences she used were:

1. All the points in his paper hung together well. His paper was very (coherent).

2. I could not understand the speaker. Her remarks were very (incoherent).

3. His paper lacked (coherency).

4. She was an (adherent) of that point of view.

5. Because of differences of opinion, the group lacks (cohesiveness).

Words suggested were written on the board. Then the students formed into groups and competed to see which group could create an additional sentence for each of the given words and if they could locate other words structurally related to *cohesion* and *adhesion*. Each group used a dictionary to assist in the sentence writing and word location.

A Model for Teaching Vocabulary in the Content Areas

Ms. Stone's lesson sequence provides a model consisting of five major components for developing vocabulary in the content areas: 1) talking with words; 2) seeing words; 3) reading words; 4) writing with words; and 5) extending word relationships.

Talking with Words

Vocabulary development is fundamentally a process of building and refining (assimilating and accommodating) word meanings so that one can use them in reading and communicating. If vocabulary is to develop, students need numerous opportunities to hear and try out new words. Through hearing and trying out, students learn to pronounce words and to use them in normal communication.

In the content areas this means that students should be asked early in the lesson sequence to do lots of describing, telling why, and telling how, especially in reference to firsthand situations. As part of the ensuing interaction, the teacher injects the technical words necessary to explain concepts and phenomena. Students pick up their teacher's words and begin to use them when talking about content they are studying.

Firsthand situations in which students can be active participants are good settings for "talking with words." In science, such situations can be simple experiments that students observe and discuss. As they do so, they begin to use the technical terms and attach meaning to them. In social studies, field trips and role playing can serve as the vehicles for "talking with words," especially with young children who need concrete experiences to understand relationships.

43

Seeing Words

As students are using their new understanding of technical terms to describe and explain, they need to "see" those terms in printed form. Such terms should be written clearly on the board or on chart paper to show their syllable pattern. Words that are structurally related can be listed one beneath the other to show those relationships. For example, *adhesive* might be listed first, with other related words below it to show the common prefix, as shown here:

ad he sive

ad he sion

ad here

ad her ing

This is an appropriate time to talk about the prefix *ad-*, meaning "to," and to practice spelling the terms. The teacher might ask, "Why is the final *e* dropped when adding *ing* in *adhering*?"

Once students have considered the group of words related to *adhesive*, they can remove the *ad-* prefix and substitute *co-*. Now is the time to talk about the meaning of *co-* and the meaning of *-sion*. It is also the time to reinforce the teaching of how to add *-ed* and *-ing* to verb forms.

When students are uncertain about spelling, they can run a quick dictionary check. All students can benefit by having a dictionary available at their desks. If this is not possible, one student can be assigned to run the dictionary check for the class. Students can also check their textbook glossary for help on spelling, pronunciation, and meaning.

Some means should be found for students to keep on file the words they will need for later reading, writing, and reviewing. The Technical Vocabulary Card described earlier is one example. Such cards can be arranged alphabetically or they can be organized by the particular unit being studied and referred to when writing on the topic or reviewing for a test.

An alternative to the word card is the personal glossary. As part of unit study, each youngster develops a notebook with a glossary at the back with a section for each letter of the alphabet. As students encounter new words, they record them with definitions and related words on the appropriate glossary page in their notebooks.

Reading for Meaning

Once students have talked about basic concepts and become familiar with new terminology, they are ready to begin reading to gather information. Using textbook reading assignments at this point will reinforce learnings and supply added examples for building concepts. Experienced teachers find that if reading is done after much discussion and after becoming familiar with new terminology, students can bring their prior knowledge to bear on their reading, and will be able to make inferences and project generalizations. Also, being familiar with new terminology, students will find the reading easier to comprehend.

Writing with Words

If young people are to develop their word power, they must use new vocabulary in their writing. Chapter 3 details strategies for incorporating writing into unit studies. At this point, suffice it to say that writing is not a single-step process. Writing requires much preliminary talking-out activity as demonstrated by Ms. Stone's lesson sequence. After the initial drafting come editing and rewriting. Then, too, as youngsters are building writing skills, they do not necessarily write alone; they can write in teacher-guided groups and in small independent writing teams.

Through writing activity students learn how to use technical terms to explain concepts in the content areas. Its value, however, is greater than that. Through writing, children can begin to master the use of connectives, transitional words, subordination, time sequence, qualification, and other sentence structure forms to express more complex relationships. In a study of sixth-grade science and social studies texts, Denis Rodgers (1974) found that connectives used very frequently included:

but	then	although	so that
if	even	while	such as
when	also	for example	too
because	perhaps	since	until
as	however	yet	whether

Mastery of more sophisticated sentence structures comes through use. As youngsters talk out relationships, cooperatively draft sentences to express these relationships, and edit what they have drafted, they are learning to use varied sentence structures to express complex relationships. In this respect, writing can have an impact on reading.

Since many technical terms are derivatives of commonly used words, learning such terms can lead to general vocabulary growth if the teacher makes the connection between technical and common meanings. We saw this in Ms. Stone's lesson when she made the connection between *cohesion* as it applies to molecular forces and such general words as *coherent, incoherency.* and *cohesiveness.* This applies to content study at all levels. First graders in American Book's social studies series study "The Self." Related words, to develop orally as part of this study, include *selfish* and *selfless.* Also, students can form words by placing *self* after *him* or *her* (*himself, herself*) or by placing *self* and a hyphen in front of other words (*self-centered* and *self-confident*). In the same way, sixth graders can build words around the root *-gram* as part of their study of communication. Making the word connection, they can consider the meanings of *pictogram, phonogram, telegram,* and even *electrocardiogram.*

Figure 7 shows how vocabulary development can be a learning goal in content study. Emphasizing vocabulary growth does not mean less time for subject-matter learning. To the contrary, if youngsters can talk and write about the content they are studying, using the precise vocabulary of the discipline, they are demonstrating mastery of that content. Every lesson in content study has the potential for building word power in the form of enlarged language meanings, increased ability to figure out word meanings, and increased ability to use the dictionary.

Strategies For Building Vocabulary Through Content Studies

Vocabulary development in content studies should begin in the primary grades, even as early as kindergarten. In this section, we shall identify strategies for building word power in the primary grades and then show how these strategies can be modified for the upper elementary and junior high school levels.

Figure 7   A MODEL FOR INCORPORATING VOCABULARY DEVELOPMENT IN CONTENT STUDY

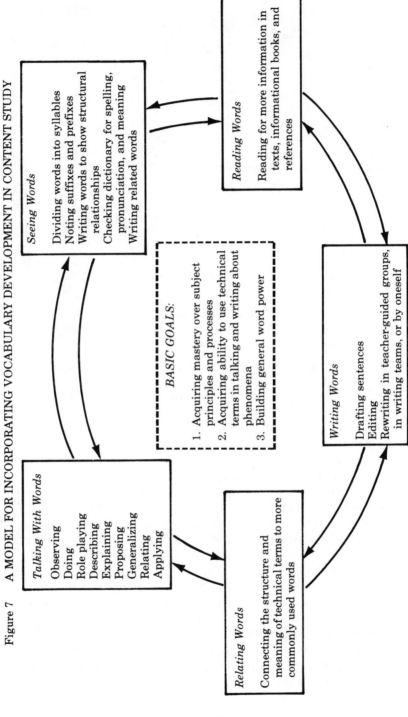

Seeing Words

Dividing words into syllables
Noting suffixes and prefixes
Writing words to show structural relationships
Checking dictionary for spelling, pronunciation, and meaning
Writing related words

Reading Words

Reading for more information in texts, informational books, and references

BASIC GOALS:

1. Acquiring mastery over subject principles and processes
2. Acquiring ability to use technical terms in talking and writing about phenomena
3. Building general word power

Writing Words

Drafting sentences
Editing
Rewriting in teacher-guided groups, in writing teams, or by oneself

Talking With Words

Observing
Doing
Role playing
Describing
Explaining
Proposing
Generalizing
Relating
Applying

Relating Words

Connecting the structure and meaning of technical terms to more commonly used words

47

Alison Gherris

The Salt Marsh
There are jelly fish, squids, crabs, tadpoles, starfish, oysters, and worms in the salt marsh.

Vocabulary Development in the Primary Grades

Strategies appropriate for the primary grades include picture sequences, pictures without words, pictures with words, picture collages, personal glossaries, bulletin board glossaries, and experience charts.

Picture Sequences. Textbook used in first- and second-grade science, social studies, and health programs generally include picture sequences, with a question or two to stimulate discussion. Using these pictures, the teacher involves children in discussion and at the same time introduces them to key terms. For example, in the first-grade American Book social studies text, pictures show youngsters participating in a variety of groups. Vocabulary words to be developed by talking about these pictures include *group, member,* and *leader.* By talking about these pictures the teacher guides the children in first hearing the words, then seeing the words, reading the words, writing the words, and relating the words to others they may know. In short, all the aspects of vocabulary development described earlier can be used with the picture series found in many texts at the primary level.

As an alternative, teachers can assemble their own picture series by clipping pictures from magazines and using them as the basis for discussion out of which come new concepts and new vocabulary. Later children can search magazines for related pictures to share with the class. Also available from educational publishers are sets of study prints on various topics for use at the kindergarten level. As children talk about such pictures, they should get used to seeing key words in print in order to understand that words on paper stand for ideas.

Pictures With and Without Words. Teachers can also draw rough sketches to illustrate key terms. Once children have begun to use new terms naturally as part of their oral vocabularies, they can add labels to make pictures with words. As the pictures with words accumulate, children can refer to them later when reading and writing about a topic. For example, a first-grade unit on groups could be comprised of three pictures —a picture of a small group, a picture of a group with many members, and a picture of a group with a clear leader. Next to each picture would be the appropriate label—*group, member,* and *leader.*

Picture Collages. Children can clip pictures or draw sketches related to a unit they are studying and make a collage comprised of visuals and words. By posting the collages on the walls or suspending them as mobiles, children have a constant reminder of words to use in talking and writing.

Personal Glossaries. As part of unit study, children in the primary grades should begin to keep their own record of basic terms in the form of personal glossaries. This can be done on cards to which they add illustrative sketches, definitions, and sample sentences using the term. Later, as they move into upper elementary grades, students might develop a glossary at the back of a notebook devoted to the unit study. Compilation of personal vocabulary lists to use for review purposes is a good study technique.

Bulletin Board Glossaries. In addition to personal glossaries, children can make a large-scale version of their cards as a bulletin-board glossary. Using light colored construction paper, children write the word, divide it into syllables, give its definition, and draw a sketch if appropriate. One full bulletin board can be reserved for the glossary of key words that relate to a unit of study. As the unit changes the glossary will change. As a variation of the bulletin board glossary, some teachers prepare 26 charts, one for each letter of the alphabet. They mount these charts in alphabetical order beneath the chalkboards.

As youngsters encounter unfamiliar words in their unit, they add these to the appropriate chart. Because so many words are likely to appear on the charts, it is impossible to include definitions, but the charts can serve as a reminder of the spelling, which will be helpful as youngsters write.

Experience Charts. Even in the primary grades, children should have the opportunity to use their developing technical vocabulary by writing. Writing occurs after children have talked about ideas, listened to ideas, and viewed ideas in pictorial form. In this respect, it serves a summarizing function; youngsters propose sentences that pull together the big ideas they have been considering. Initially, writing at the primary level takes the form of experience charts dictated to the teacher, who records the child's words on large chart paper. If charts are kept on an easel, they can be reread on successive days with children learning to read key terms in a context meaningful to them. Some teachers record key words associated with unit study in a colored flo-pen that is different from the rest of the narrative. In this way, the key words stand out to be used by children as they begin to write independently.

Asking young children to dictate on social studies and science topics does not result in an experience chart in the usual sense, because what they dictate does not come from their personal experience. If, however, first graders have had considerable discussion on a topic such as life in deserts and have seen numerous pictures, writing is feasible. Children can dictate about what kinds of plants live on the desert and why these plants live there; about how people's lifestyles differ in the desert; even about why there are deserts. Children's vicarious experiences with deserts have given them the necessary background to share a lot of information.

Vocabulary Development in the Upper Grades

As children move into the upper grades and beyond, they are faced with heavier reading loads, and their science and social studies texts become increasingly complex. At this stage, they must become independent in figuring out new vocabulary by using contextual and structural clues. Here are a few strategies to help children build their word analysis skills.

Teacher-guided Analysis. In the upper elementary years, reading still requires considerable guidance; the teacher must ask questions that focus attention on contextual relationships. Dittoed sheets that provide information on a topic being studied are helpful. As students read, they can circle key terms and

50

underline definitions, synonyms, and antonyms that help them understand the basic terms in the content unit being studied. This activity prepares students for independent learning and establishes good study habits for future years when they will own their textbooks and can underline rather than take notes.

Interpreting labeled diagrams and schematics provides another opportunity for students to develop vocabulary. Here again, the teacher's job is to ask questions that direct students to think through relationships underlying key concepts and terminology. As follow-up, students can make their own labeled diagrams, writing short definitions next to labels. This approach is useful when studying content that deals with structural units, for example, the cell with cell wall and nucleus; the atom with protons, neutrons, and electrons; the heart with auricles and ventricles.

Visual Word Charts. Another vocabulary-building technique in unit study is the use of visual word charts that show word relationships. For example, in a social studies lesson the word *hemisphere,* could be put on a chart with other words containing the same root such as *sphere, spherical, troposphere,* and *spheroid.* To create such a chart, students will likely have to consult a dictionary; thus they will be building dictionary skills in the process. Similar visual word charts can be made for synonyms and antonyms and for word trees that include words derived from the same source.

Reinforcing Vocabulary Growth. One-time exposure to new terminology is not enough to make these words a part of students' functional vocabulary. The teacher needs to use these words on a continuing basis. As students hear the new terms in sentence contexts, they will assimilate them into their own word banks and will begin to use them in classroom discussion.

There are many creative ways to reinforce vocabulary growth in the upper elementary grades. One fifth-grade teacher had the children make three puppets to use in the study of rocks in a geology unit. One puppet was named "Mr. Igneous," another "Ms. Metamorphic," and another "Ms. Sedimentary." Youngsters took turns speaking through the puppets and told as much information about that kind of rock as they could remember. As the class learned more about the different kinds of rocks, the amount of information to be told increased. This provided an opportunity for several children to take turns with each of the puppets to review all of the information. In the process of retelling what they had learned, students had to use all the geologic terms they had learned.

This type of oral review activity can occur in a variety of contexts. In studying the American Revolution, students can take turns speaking from the viewpoint of the British and then for the Americans, using a puppet head of King George III and one of George Washington. In the same way, in a science unit about how the body works, students can make hand puppets representing the heart, lung, kidneys, etc. and speak through the puppets to explain how essential organs function and how they are related. The result can be a playlet involving all the children as they learn content, practice new terminology, and have fun in the process.

Vocabulary Growth Through Group Activity. In unit studies, especially at upper grade levels, group activity provides many opportunities for vocabulary growth. Working in teams or talk-'ing together in small discussion groups, students hear both common and technical terms used in a meaningful way. By first using terms orally, students find follow-up reading easier. Prior to group discussion, many teachers list on the board the key terms related to the topic and have the class pronounce these terms. There are a number of ways to organize small-group activity in unit study that will facilitate vocabulary development:

1. Each student in a group is given a specific assignment. Then the group members come together and each reports on his or her findings. The group then develops an outline that includes all the findings.

2. The group is given a series of discussion questions, and the group members work cooperatively to answer the questions.

3. Two smaller groups merge to check their answers and come up with a compromise when there is disagreement.

4. Students revolve from one group to another. In each group the same questions are considered as in the previous group. This deliberate repetition provides for additional input by the new group member and at the same time provides reinforcement of key terms relevant to the question.

A natural outgrowth of group activity is sharing with the total class or with other members of the group. If properly structured, this sharing can lead to vocabulary development. Students will hear their classmates using new terms in oral reporting and later will themselves use these terms in discussions that grow out of the reporting sessions.

Oral reporting, however, can often be a deadly affair. To avoid this, a teacher should help children develop their oral presentation skills, i.e., to speak clearly; to emphasize key points; to use visuals to clarify a concept; to make effective use of pauses, facial expressions, eye contact, and gestures; to speak from brief notes rather than from a written report.

The teacher can also structure oral reporting to provide variety. Some possibilities are:

1. As dialogues in which two students report in tandem on a topic; first one student makes a point, then the other, passing the reporting task back and forth between them.

2. As forums in which the members of a team each report a part of the total presentation within a time limit.

3. As total class general discussions in which youngsters contribute their findings informally.

4. As dramatizations.

In each of these instances, whatever the format, the key to successful reporting is active involvement. Listeners must be directed to ask questions. In asking questions and offering reactions, students are involved in the subject content and are using related technical terms. In addition, they are building their oral expressive skills. With emphasis on oral involvement, students will acquire the ability to express themselves in discussions and to present oral reports that communicate in clear and interesting fashion to others.

Summary

This chapter has provided an instructional model for helping youngsters build their word power as part of content learning. This model has five components: 1) Talking with Words; 2) Seeing Words; 3) Reading Words; 4) Writing with Words; and 5) Extending Word Relationships. In sum, to teach vocabulary across the curriculum, the teacher must actively involve youngsters in talking and listening, in reading and writing. Only through active use will youngsters build the meanings being communicated by everyday words and technical terms; only through active use will youngsters incorporate words into their functional vocabularies.

Related References

Dale, Edgar. *The Word Game: Improving Communications.* Bloomington, Ind.: Phi Delta Kappa, 1975.

Deighton, Lee. *Vocabulary Development in the Classroom.* New York: Teachers College Press, 1959.

Gaskins, Irene. "Reading for Learning: Going Beyond Basals in the Elementary Grades." *Reading Teacher* 35 (1981):323-328.

Glaus, Marlene. *From Thoughts to Words.* Urbana, Ill.: National Council of Teachers of English, 1965.

Johnson, D. D. and Pearson, P. David. *Teaching Reading Vocabulary.* New York: Holt, Rinehart and Winston, 1978.

Jones, Linda. "An Interactive View of Reading: Implications for the Classroom." *Reading Teacher* 35 (1982):772-777.

Lunstrum, John and Taylor, Bob. *Teaching Reading in the Social Studies.* Newark, Del.: International Reading Association, 1978.

Preston, Ralph, ed. *A New Look at Reading in the Social Studies.* Newark, Del.: International Reading Association, 1969.

Rodgers, Denis. "Which Connectives? Signals to Enhance Comprehension." *Journal of Reading* 17 (1974):466.

Smith, Nila and Robinson, H. Allan. "Extending Knowledge of Word Meanings." In *Reading Instruction for Today's Children.* Englewood Cliffs, N.J.: Prentice-Hall, 1980.

Thelen, Judith. *Improving Reading in Science.* Newark, Del.: International Reading Association, 1976.

Tovey, Duane. "Inseparable 'Language and Content' Instruction." *Journal of Reading* 22 (1979):720-725.

Making Candles

A long time ago candles were used to light people's houses. Candles were made mostly like they are today. Candles were made like this. First they got a wick. Then they took some tallow and put it into a boiling kettle. Then they dipped the wick into the tallow. They dipped it in many times. The tallow started getting thicker and thicker around the wick.

3

Writing Across the Curriculum

Composition is, for the most part, an effort of slow diligence and steady perseverance, to which the mind is dragged by necessity or resolution.

Samuel Johnson,
The Adventurer

Artwork and text contributed by
Ari Globerman

Writing Across the Curriculum

If students are to express themselves skillfully, even as they learn the essential facts, concepts, and generalizations within the various disciplines, there must be many opportunities for writing across the curriculum. Within the content areas, the connection between writing and reading can be made, for most of the thinking skills used in reading are the same as those used in written expression. The challenge facing teachers is how to integrate writing into daily lessons and unit plans of content studies. In this chapter we shall:
1. Describe writing skills to be acquired and present a checklist of skills;
2. Present a design for content lesson sequences that incorporates writing activity and connects writing with reading;
3. Describe specific strategies for teaching writing from the primary to the upper grades.

Thinking/Writing Skills to be Acquired

To write well is to formulate worthwhile ideas into sentences and paragraphs that communicate with clarity and force. Perceived in this way, writing is first of all a thinking process, a way of dealing with content to express new relationships. It is also a craft, a way of styling words so that they create a lasting impression. To teach writing, one must be concerned with both content and craft.

Modes of Writing

Content is communicated through different modes of thinking/writing. Some content requires a *reflective* mode of thinking; it describes what the writer has observed, heard, or read. It may require the writer to report on events, to tell how to do something, to retell something heard or read, or to summarize. Reflective writing requires a particular style of thinking.

A second kind of content deals with relationships. To write about this kind of content, the writer must think in *relational* ways. The writer must compare and contrast, identify how two or more items are the same or different, and classify, analyze, or explain events or items.

A third mode of thinking, called *projective,* requires the writer to propose ideas that go beyond observable data. A writer who predicts, guesses, generalizes, designs plans for action, or devises original classification schemes, is thinking in the projective mode.

A fourth mode of thinking might be called *personal.* Here the writer expresses feelings, preferences, beliefs, or judgments. Many different forms of writing require this mode of thinking, particularly poems, editorials, or essays.

At times writing calls for a fifth kind of thinking, best described as *inventive.* Here the writer must be truly original in creating descriptions, dialogue, characters, and plots. This clearly is the stuff of short stories, fables, myths, tall tales, and narrative poems. At times the inventive mode shows up in informational writing when a writer composes vignettes or anecdotes to illustrate a point.

Identifying the different modes of thought is not to suggest that a particular writing task requires only one mode of thought. In composing a piece, the writer may well begin by describing observations, then shift to relational thinking to contrast and compare these observations. Sometimes within a single paragraph, a writer may shift modes, for example, by making a series of specific observations and then concluding with a generalization about them. The notion that different kinds of writing call for different modes of thought does, however, suggest to the teacher a variety of ways to structure the writing curriculum. A complete writing program should provide students with the opportunity to think in the reflective, relational, projective, personalized, and inventive modes.

Figure 8 is a checklist of thinking/writing skills that can serve as a diagnostic instrument for evaluating students' growth and as a guide for designing a comprehensive and developmental writing program. The teacher must progressively structure more sophisticated activities that lead to growth in these skills, keeping in mind the various stages of cognitive development and the elementary child's need for concrete experiences in order to generalize, hypothesize, and predict.

Science and social studies teachers often talk about teaching youngsters to think in the modes of their disciplines. Observing and describing, retelling, summarizing, relating, hypothesizing, generalizing, designing, and even personalizing and inventing are what study in these areas is all about. These modes of thinking are the same as those required to write about content in science and social studies.

59

Figure 8   A CHECKLIST OF THINKING/WRITING SKILLS*

The student is able to:	high skill	medium skill	low skill	no skill
A. Reflect on the world by representing with accuracy what was observed, heard, or read.				
1. Describe the characteristics of things observed.				
2. Report on a happening by telling who, when, where, what, under what conditions.				
3. Tell how to do something or go somewhere.				
4. Retell in own words ideas heard or read.				
5. Summarize key points in shortened form.				
B. Relate phenomena.				
1. Compare items and ideas.				
2. Contrast items and ideas.				
3. Classify or group items that share a property.				
4. Analyze by ordering items in terms of size, position, or complexity.				
5. Analyze by ordering items sequentially or chronologically.				
6. Explain why or how something happened.				
C. Project ideas that go beyond observable data.				
1. Hypothesize, predict, or guess based on data given.				
2. Propose generalizations that explain relationships.				
3. Design or set forth a scheme for classifying data, taking action, or planning.				

(continued on page 61)

60

Figure 8 (cont.)

D. Personalize.

1. Express feelings about an event, person, or thing.
2. Express a preference, or a liking or disliking for something.
3. Express an opinion or a personal belief.
4. Render a judgment and support that judgment by referring to clearly defined criteria.

E. Invent

1. Create original descriptions.
2. Create dialogue as part of writing.
3. Create characters.
4. Create plots.

Student's Name: _____ Date: _____

Teacher's Name: _____

Student's Comments:

*Based on categories of writing from Hennings and Grant, *Written Expression in the Language Arts,* (Teachers College Press, 1981).

Subject matter teachers have traditionally relied on reading and discussion to help students comprehend content. They ask students to read to find out, to talk about ideas before and after reading, and to listen to content. Writing belongs within this instructional framework. The "writing connection" logically is the next step, because it is through such integration of communication skills that children acquire understanding of the content areas.

The Writing Craft

The craft of writing involves drafting ideas on paper so that they communicate clearly. Looking at writing in these terms, one is first concerned with the selection of words and the design of sentences and paragraphs. Good writers must select just the right verb, adjective, or adverb to communicate the intended message. They must be able to manipulate a variety of sentence patterns and draw from a repertoire of transitional words to express the appropriate relationships. They must be able to sequence their thoughts logically and to develop paragraphs that focus on a main idea. Organizing ideas for writing is a thinking process in and of itself.

Other aspects of the writing craft involve the numerous language conventions, such as capitalization, punctuation, and spelling. Although these language conventions are not as important to communication as deeper thinking patterns, students must acquire skill in them if their writing is to be acceptable by customary standards.

Figure 9 provides a checklist of writing skills that can be used for diagnostic purposes. It is apparent that these skills cannot be taught only in English and language arts classes. If students are to express themselves with force and clarity, they must have opportunities for writing in every curriculum area at every level.

Writing is not only a skill but is also an instructional strategy, a means of acquiring understanding of basic concepts and generalizations within the content areas. Writing can also serve a diagnostic function. Students who read on a topic and then write about it provide the teacher with information on whether they really understand the topic, whether they see relationships between a main idea and subordinate points, whether they can draw conclusions based on the information read, and whether they can apply their understanding in explaining or interpreting a related situation. From students' writing, the teacher learns whether more work with the basic facts, concepts, and generalizations is needed.

Figure 9   A CHECKLIST OF WRITING SKILLS

The student is able to:	high skill	medium skill	low skill	no skill
A. Organize ideas into related wholes:				
1. Compose paragraphs that focus on one main topic.				
2. Compose paragraphs in which points develop logically.				

(continued on page 63)

Figure 9 (cont.)

3. Use words that communicate sequential relationships: *first, then, after that, finally.*
4. Use words that communicate contrasting relationships: *on the other hand, in this case, in that case.*
5. Use words that communicate cause and effect relationships: *as a result, therefore, thus, accordingly.*
6. Use words that communicate comparable relationships: *in the same way, similarly.*
7. Sequence a series of paragraphs so that ideas develop progressively.

B. Compose in meaningful sentence units:

1. Write complete sentences, not run-ons and fragments.
2. Avoid connecting sentence thoughts with a string of *ands.*
3. Combine thoughts by subordinating ideas.

C. Handle basic punctuation/ capitalization patterns important in clear communication of meaning:

End sentence punctuation, addresses, dates, appositives, parenthetical expressions, direct address, direct conversation and quotations, combined sentences, imbedded sentences.

D. Select words that communicate with force and clarity:

1. Use appropriate synonyms.
2. Avoid wordiness.

A Design for Teaching Writing in Content Areas

How can writing be taught while dealing with fundamental concepts and generalizations in the content areas? This section presents an instructional design by 1) offering a case study of a classroom situation in which writing is an integral component, 2) giving a generalized model of instruction, and 3) suggesting a variety of contexts in which this model can be applied.

Writing in the Content Areas: A Case Study

It was the third week in September, and students in Bruce Raspolitch's fifth grade were well into their first social studies unit that dealt with the North American continent—its regions, rivers, and nations.

On the previous day, students had read the section in their text that briefly describes the rivers and lakes of North America. Now Mr. Raspolitch asked them to look at a table that lists the major rivers and their lengths in kilometers and miles. (See below).

Largest Rivers in North America

Rivers	Length in KM	Length in Miles
Mackenzie	4,216	2,530
Mississippi	3,757	2,254
Missouri	3,704	2,222
St. Lawrence	3,040	1,824
Rio Grande	3,016	1,810
Yukon	2,880	1,728
Arkansas	2,320	1,392
Colorado	2,320	1,392
Columbia	1,942	1,165
Saskatchewan	1,928	1,157
Peace	1,912	1,147
Snake	1,661	1,032
Red	1,629	1,012

Working with a wall map of North America, student volunteers traced the paths of the listed rivers from their sources to their mouths and described the geographic regions through which they passed. As students identified the rivers on the wall map, the rest of the class used desk maps to label the rivers and their lengths. When the class had labeled the major rivers, Mr. Raspolitch shifted gears by asking, "What is the main idea communicated by the table in our book?"

Craig was quick to respond, "That the Mackenzie River is the biggest river."

Mr. Raspolitch replied, "Craig has not really given us the main idea of the table. He has supplied us with one piece of information. Let's look again and use the caption on the table as a clue to the main idea." This time Keith responded, "There are lots of large rivers in North America."

"Exactly," answered Mr. Raspolitch. "Keith, come up and record your sentence as the first one in a general paragraph about North American rivers that we are going to write together."

When Keith had recorded his sentence on the board, Raspolitch returned to Craig. "Craig, can you take the point you previously made and express it as a second sentence in the paragraph?" Craig agreed and wrote on the board, *The biggest river is the Mackenzie River.*

At that point Mr. Raspolitch asked students to contribute another sentence to their paragraph that supported the idea that there are lots of large rivers in North America. Three students volunteered sentences. The paragraph on the board now looked like this:

> There are lots of large rivers in North America. The biggest river is the Mackenzie River. Another big river is the Mississippi. Then the Missouri. The St. Lawrence River is 3,040 kilometers.

As with most first drafts, the paragraph needed rewriting. So Mr. Raspolitch began by telling students to look at their first sentence and then asked, "Can we rewrite our sentence to avoid starting with *There*? Let's keep away from *there* if we can. It is not a strong way to begin." The students suggested several different beginning sentences. They finally agreed on *Many large rivers flow across the North American continent.*

"Let's look at our second sentence," Mr. Raspolitch continued, "and see if we can find a word that is repetitious." The class readily agreed that the second *river* was unnecessary. Then Raspolitch asked, "Who can suggest another word for *biggest* to make it say precisely what we are talking about?"

The youngsters quickly got the point and substituted *longest* for *biggest*.

At that point Mr. Raspolitch moved from the basic facts of the paragraph to the expansion of ideas. "Who can remember a fact about the Mackenzie from our map study that we can add to our sentence to fatten it up?" This question was tougher. Students had to go back to the map and point out the Mackenzie's location again. They talked about the location and noted that it was located in northwestern Canada. The class decided that this was a significant point to add, so they rewrote their second sentence to read *The longest river is the Mackenzie, which is located in northwestern Canada.*

At this juncture, Mr. Raspolitch decided to teach sentence-combining skill. He asked, "What's wrong with *Then the Missouri* as a sentence in our paragraph?" When the fifth graders had made the point that these three words were not a sentence because there was no verb part, their teacher asked, "How are the Mississippi and the Missouri related?" The students identified a number of relationships—that they are the next longest rivers on the continent, that they are in the central United States, that the Missouri flows into the Mississippi. With these relationships established, Mr. Raspolitch asked, "Who can draft one sentence that includes information about both the Missouri and the Mississippi since these rivers are related?" After considerable discussion, the students cooperatively put together this sentence: *The Mississippi and the Missouri, both located in the center of the United States, are the next two longest rivers.*

Mr. Raspolitch's next question was, "Is there a way to add information about some other North American rivers to our last sentence to make our paragraph more informative?" Students argued about whether this could be done and how it could be done. They finally devised this sentence: *Other long North American rivers are the St. Lawrence, the Rio Grande, the Yukon, the Arkansas, and the Colorado.* The students, with no prompting, decided to include only these rivers and not to mention others from the table. Their rationale was that the other rivers were less than 2,000 kilometers long.

The class gave their paragraph a title, *Major North American Rivers,* and that ended the combined writing/social studies lesson for the day. Here is the final paragraph Mr. Raspolitch's fifth graders wrote:

Major North American Rivers

Many large rivers flow across the North American continent. The longest river is the Mackenzie, which is located in northern Canada. The Mississippi and the Missouri, both located in the center of the United States, are the next longest. Other long North American rivers are the St. Lawrence, the Rio Grande, the Yukon, the Arkansas, and the Colorado.

By comparing this final draft to the first draft, one can see how through the teacher's guidance, students can develop fluency in their writing.

The next day the fifth graders worked in small teams to expand the data from the table in their books to include information about the river locations, the source of each river, the body of water into which each flows, and the general direction of river flow. Students obtained this information from a large wall map and from a map of North America in their text. They compiled their data directly onto a chart like the one in figure 10.

Figure 10   DATA RETRIEVAL CHART FOR WRITING

RIVER RELATIONSHIPS				
The River	*Source of the River*	*Body of Water into Which the River Flows*	*General Location of the River*	*General Direction of River Flow*
Mackenzie				
Mississippi				
Missouri				
St. Lawrence				
Rio Grande				
Yukon				
Arkansas				
Colorado				

It took a full period for students to complete their data retrieval charts. The next day the small teams shared their findings to insure that all groups had complete and accurate information that would later be used for writing paragraphs.

67

In a follow-up session, students gathered in writing/rewriting teams. Each team pulled a slip containing a river name from a box. Working from their data retrieval charts, each composed a paragraph describing the river it had selected. After the teams had drafted their paragraphs, they exchanged them with another team. Rewriting consisted of adding information, sharpening the introductory sentence, combining sentences to make them flow better, substituting stronger words, and checking spelling punctuation, and capitalization.

On successive days, Mr. Raspolitch's fifth graders continued to explore the water system of North America. At one point they hypothesized about the role that the lakes and rivers played in the economic development of the continent, and they brainstormed a list of ways the water system had been an asset in this development. Students cooperatively compiled a chart of what they called "River Contributions." Later, students individually wrote a paragraph incorporating the ideas about river contributions that they had charted and discussed.

A Design for Teaching Writing in the Content Areas

Mr. Raspolitch's lesson series suggests a sequence useful in teaching writing within content areas. This sequence includes prewriting, drafting, and rewriting, and involves students in reading, listening, and speaking. It also includes three forms of writing: teacher-guided group writing, small group collaborative writing, and individual writing.

Prewriting. Numerous researchers have investigated instructional approaches to improve students' writing. Summarizing much of this research in the *English Journal* (January 1978), Elizabeth Haynes concludes that many approaches have negative outcomes: that the study of traditional grammar is not effective in eliminating writing errors; that more writing alone does not necessarily mean better writing; and that intensive correction of student errors by the teacher is futile. On the positive side, Haynes finds favorable outcomes from prewriting activity in which talking together or talking into a tape recorder precedes writing.

James Moffett (1979) offers a possible explanation as to why oral activity that precedes drafting of ideas on paper has a positive impact on writing quality. According to Moffett, when people write they are essentially involved in first talking to themselves. Writers taste words on their tongues, hear sentences in their mind's eye, and edit or discard possibilities as they occur.

This is all part of inner speech, or of thought itself.

From this point of view, activities that trigger talking to one's self in one's head, or inner speech, will have a positive effect on one's ability to compose ideas on paper. These activities include games, practical problems to solve, imagining, and dialogue with others. Moffett also suggests that lots of good conversation, when interiorized, becomes part of inner speech. In the context of science and social studies such prewriting activities may include brainstorming, categorizing ideas, compiling data retrieval charts in groups, talking around a problem to clarify relationships, and sharing ideas in small writing teams.

Drafting. The process of drafting sentences and paragraphs can proceed orally through teacher-guided group writing. In group writing the teacher guides the students in thinking through ideas before cooperatively drafting sentences and organizing related ideas into paragraphs. During the group composition period the teacher asks questions that lead students to express relationships they perceive from the data and even to choose words that express those relationships clearly. Sharply focused teacher questions prepare students for the inner thinking, or speaking, that must go on when they compose individually.

Collaborative writing also encourages students to think through relationships prior to composing. When young people must function cooperatively in a small writing team to compose a paragraph or two, they are forced to talk out their ideas —to think out loud, so to speak. In sharing ideas with others in a small group, young writers begin to use the technical vocabulary needed to express relationships in the content areas—vocabulary that they go on to use naturally when composing individually.

Individual composing flows naturally from group writing experiences. When students have cooperated on writing on topics about which much preliminary brainstorming, charting, and talking together have taken place, they will see their individual compositions as an extension of the cooperative writing they have already done and approach it with considerably more confidence. Individual writing gives the teacher an opportunity to diagnose children's developing writing ability.

Editing and Revising. Experienced teachers know that children often balk at going back to rewrite. To them, once drafted, a piece is done! However, even the most able writers return to edit and revise what they have drafted. Children should be involved in rewriting, so it becomes an expected part of their writing activity. Teacher-guided group rewriting, as demonstrated by Mr. Raspolitch, can help young writers to understand that rewriting is an integral part of writing. Guided by questions raised by their teacher, students edit and revise. In revising, they may delete some points and insert additional information; in so doing they may have to create more complex sentence patterns. They may substitute more forceful words and vary sentence patterns. In editing, they check to see that sentences are complete, punctuation and capitalization are appropriate, and words are spelled correctly.

Of course, with student rewriting a teacher would not try to deal with all these points. Looking at a paragraph just drafted cooperatively, teachers must make a decision as to which points to stress, depending on the writing problems apparent in the piece or on the particular skills that are being taught at that point.

In making decisions about editing and revising, teachers can be guided by research on how to help children become more sophisticated writers. Mellon (1969) has demonstrated that with practice students can be helped to overcome their tendency to string sentences together with the word *and*. In a later study, O'Hare (1973) got similar results, as did Combs (1976) and Perron (1976). Reviewing the findings of the early studies in this area, Stotsky (1975) commented that "sentence-combining practice will increase both syntactic maturity and overall quality in the writing of upper elementary and junior high school students."

These studies suggest that during teacher-guided group writing, starting about grade three when children begin to write longer pieces, the teacher can begin to work systematically on rewriting. She might ask, "Look at this sentence: *The Mackenzie River is the longest river and it is in Canada and it flows north.* How can we rewrite it to avoid the *ands*? Who can take the first two sentence parts (*The Mackenzie River is the longest river and it is in Canada*) and put them together without the *and*?" Especially helpful here is the sentence-lifting technique in which the teacher writes the original sentence in big print on construction paper. Students use scissors to cut the sentence into its three component parts, and then reconstruct it without the *ands*.

Similar rewriting techniques can be part of collaborative writing. A team can rewrite a short piece that it has cooperatively written on a previous day. Having a day between the writing and the rewriting is often helpful because the students return to their pieces with a fresh eye. An alternative is to exchange papers between teams, with each team giving suggestions for rewriting to the other team. In either case, experienced teachers have found that giving students specific rewriting assignments encourages careful editing and revision.

Depending on the skills the teacher wishes to emphasize, appropriate assignments include:

1. Deleting at least one unnecessary word.

2. Adding at least one additional piece of information to an existing sentence.

3. Combining two smaller sentences into one without using the word *and*. Use *who, which, that, when, because, so, if, while, as, since* as possible connectives.

4. Substituting one stronger word for a word used in the first draft.

5. Identifying the main idea of each paragraph and checking that every sentence in a paragraph contributes to that idea.

When students compose individually, the teacher/student conference provides a good setting in which to encourage rewriting. Have students select a piece or two from several they have drafted and ask them to rewrite these pieces for sharing with others—in a sense, for publication. Appropriate questions a teacher might raise relate to the logic of the sentence order, the relationship of specific sentences to the main idea of the paragraph, the possibility of combining sentences, addition of words to make sentence meaning more precise, or insertion of punctuation to clarify relationships. Although the teacher conference is time consuming, it can be done while other students continue to write on their own or as part of small writing-rewriting teams.

Writing is not simply the process of taking pen in hand and drafting ideas on paper; it requires both prewriting and rewriting activity. Accordingly, when designing writing-thinking activity in the content areas, the teacher must structure writing sequences to include opportunities for prewriting, for drafting, and for rewriting. Figure 11 presents a model for designing writing sequences in the content areas. The model suggests that writing in the content areas is a multifaceted activity that includes reading, listening, viewing, doing, talking, sharing, and, above all, thinking.

Contexts for Writing in the Content Areas

The fields of science and social studies rely heavily on visuals to summarize content or to illustrate concepts. From the earliest grades most social studies and science texts are filled with

Figure 11   MODEL FOR DESIGNING WRITING SEQUENCES IN THE
CONTENT AREAS

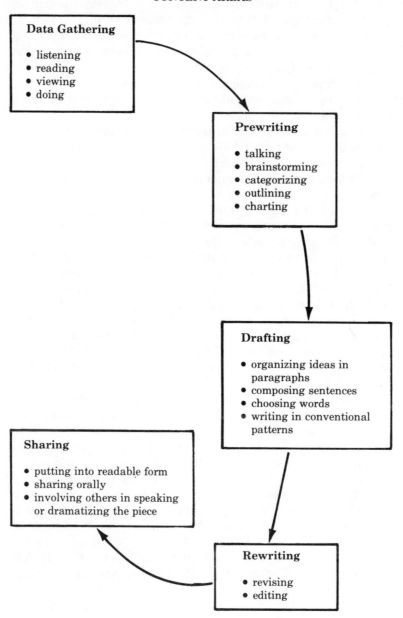

visuals—maps, graphs, charts, diagrams, schematics, pictures —that can provide the content for students' writing.

From Visuals into Writing. Following are some specific activities using visuals as a source for writing:

1. Ask students to analyze pictures in their social studies texts to find out how education, dress, agriculture, architecture, or any other feature of the culture being depicted differ from their own. Have students talk out the differences and then in a teacher-guided group writing session, express those differences in a paragraph and then rewrite. Later, in writing teams, have students handle a related picture in the same way. Last, have students write individual paragraphs.

2. Ask students to study a graph, such as one showing energy consumption and production in the United States over a 50-year period. After considerable discussion, have students express the points raised by composing a single paragraph of explanation.

3. Ask students key questions about relationships depicted on a map, such as one showing the major exploration patterns during the fifteenth and sixteenth centuries. Follow up with a group or individual writing assignment that discusses the relationships noted.

4. Involve students in a discussion of data in a table or chart, such as the statistics on immigration patterns in the seventeenth and eighteenth centuries. After reaching some generalizations through discussion, record them in paragraph form.

From Reading into Writing. Reading naturally leads into writing, which can begin with even very young children. In the primary grades, textbooks not only provide information but pose questions as part of the textual matter. These questions, which are generally intended for discussion purposes, can also serve as topics for paragraph drafting. For example, a first-grade science text (*Concepts in Science,* Harcourt Brace Jovanovich) shows three pictures: the first is an ice cube on a fork balanced above a glass; the second is the cube partially melted with some water in the glass; and the third is a wet fork and a glass now with more water. The text asks, "How does the ice change?" The teacher's guide suggests that youngsters describe each picture and talk in terms of the ice melting. The first-grade teacher, who wants to build writing skills simultaneously as youngsters acquire concepts, can begin by having youngsters dictate sentences that tell step-by-step how the ice changes. The teacher, serving as scribe, records those sentences on the chalkboard or on chart paper. Later teacher and children go back to rewrite their sentences to form a cohesive paragraph.

In the same text, another picture series shows a glass of ice cubes on a sunny window sill. A clock nearby reads 9:00. A second picture shows the same glass, now filled with water on the same sunny window sill, and the clock now reads 11:00. The text asks the question: "Why does the ice change?" The teacher's guide suggests talking with the children about such factors as the passage of time and the sunny location in order to hypothesize possible causes. Here again, the teacher interested in writing skills can use the activity as a springboard to writing. With teacher guidance, youngsters dictate sentences—perhaps only two or three—explaining why.

From Doing into Writing. Writing can also be an outgrowth of hands-on experiences that occur as part of content learning. Simple investigations, such as the ones with melting ice cubes described above, can be performed by the children themselves. Talk, of course, is an integral part of the prewriting experience with students describing what they did, listing the materials they used, and describing what happened as a result. Drafting comes next. Youngsters can cooperatively compose paragraphs under such headings as "Procedures We Followed," "Materials We Used," and "Results We Observed." Then children can brainstorm possible explanations of what happened and draft a fourth paragraph under the heading "Our Explanation of Why This Happened."

From Viewing into Writing. In much the same way, writing can be an outgrowth of film or filmstrip viewing. In this context, the prewriting stage consists of the viewing and the follow-up talk. After viewing, the students recall as many facts as they remember from the film. They record these facts on the chalkboard, categorize them according to subtopics, and then write paragraphs based on the information they have organized. On pages 82-85, the reader will find a more detailed description of this kind of lesson sequence that includes data gathering, data organizing, and paragraph drafting.

Specific Strategies for Teaching Writing in the Content Areas

In teaching writing as part of content learning, the teacher must use techniques appropriate to the child's developmental level. At one level is the young child who is just learning to read and make the letters of the alphabet. At another level is the older student who has learned the basic writing skills but needs assistance in drafting clear, well-organized sentences and paragraphs. The sections that follow provide some suggestions for teaching writing at various developmental levels.

The Beginning Writer—Building Rudimentary Recording Skills

Specific strategies for teaching writing to young children as part of content learning include group dictation and rewriting, individual dictation and tracing over, individual dictation and writing over, composition of repetitive pieces, composition of framed paragraphs, word charting, and creative spelling.

Group Dictation and Rewriting. In kindergartens and first grades, group dictation of ideas is a proven strategy for developing early reading and writing skills. The teacher gathers the children into a conversation group and encourages them to talk about classroom events, holidays they anticipate, excursions they have taken together, a story they have heard, or a filmstrip they have viewed. After spending considerable time in this prewriting activity, the teacher then asks children to give sentences that tell about the events just discussed. Usually the teacher asks for only three or four sentences and records them in large script and in paragraph form on a chart. At this point the teacher reads the sentences dictated, passing her hand from left to right under the dictated words. The teacher then reads the sentences again, this time asking youngsters to chorus the lines aloud. After several group repetitions, individual children try to read a sentence or two aloud.

As part of the group dictation, there are several strategies the teacher can use to help children develop beginning writing skills. These include:

1. *Introducing the sentence.* From the beginning, the teacher should use the word *sentence:* "Who can give me a sentence that tells what we saw when we visited the bank?" Having recorded several sentences that the children suggest, the teacher continues, "Let's look at how all our sentences begin. What kind of a letter do we use to begin a sentence? What do we put at the end of each sentence?" Later as children dictate sentences, the teacher may ask one youngster to write the capital letter at the beginning of a sentence, and another youngster to add the period at the end of the sentence.

2. *Introducing the paragraph.* From the beginning, the teacher should follow paragraphing conventions in recording sentences children dictate. This means recording the sentences in paragraph form with the first word indented. In introducing a writing activity, the teacher uses the word *paragraph*, "Let's write a paragraph that tells about our trip to the businesses in our town."

3. *Introducing the notion of logical flow of ideas.* As youngsters become comfortable with the process of group dictation, the teacher can take the sentences the children have dictated and cut them into individual strips. Now the teacher asks, "Let's look at our sentences. Which one do you think would make the best first sentence in our paragraph so that the reader knows right away what the main point of our paragraph is?" Students reorganize the sentences so that the paragraph is more logical than in the first draft. As youngsters dictate other paragraphs, reorganizing sentences becomes a natural part of the experience. Guided by teacher questions, youngsters decide on what is the best sentence order. The teacher then numbers the sentences to indicate the order in which they will be read. In early grades, where children practice penmanship skills by making individual copies of a group dictation, they copy the sentences in the order indicated by the numbers. This is their introduction to the process of rewriting.

4. *Introducing transitional words to show logical sentence sequences.* To introduce children to the idea of logical sentence sequence, a teacher can guide children's dictation by asking a series of questions, each of which contains a key transitional word. For example, if youngsters have just made pancakes, the teacher can begin the dictation by asking, "What big task did we do together today?" then follow with "What did we do first when we made our pancakes? What did we do next? What did we do after that?" When children respond, typically they propose sentences with the key transitional words (*today, first, next, after that*) their teacher used. The result is a clearly sequenced description of what occurred. To achieve the same purpose in upper grades, teachers can use such words as *if, as a result, in this case, in that case* when guiding group composition.

Individual Dictation and Tracing Over. Generally, children who have talked together about a topic are eager to dictate individually. To begin, ask youngsters to draw their ideas on paper. Research by Donald Graves (1975) seems to indicate that visualizing is an integral part of writing, especially with beginning writers. At the time children are drawing their ideas, the teacher moves from child to child, asking each to give one sentence that expresses the ideas he or she is depicting visually. The teacher prints the child's words lightly in pencil on the art paper. The child then traces over the teacher's letters with a crayon.

Back Yards
We saw pictures of back yards.
They had trees, birds, flowers,
squirrels, rabbits, and grass,

Individual Dictation and Copying. After some experience in tracing over words, the next step is copying a sentence the teacher has printed during individual dictation. To facilitate this copying, the teacher should write on every other line of ruled paper. The children then copy the sentences directly below those the teacher has recorded. Because recording is a laborious process for the young child just learning to form letters, teachers should restrict the dictation to two or three sentences —sentences that begin with capitals, have end punctuation, and are set on the page in paragraph form.

Individual Recording. Shortly, children are ready to record independently. At first, this poses a major problem because they may have trouble spelling even basic words. Following are some ideas for helping children to write independently:

1. *Word charting.* As youngsters talk together during prewriting activity, the teacher can focus on basic words and re-

cord these on charts that are hung around the room, with a chart for each letter of the alphabet. Some teachers number each word on the basic word charts. Then when a child asks for a word to be spelled during individual writing, the teacher can suggest, "Look at our *T t* chart. The word you want is number 3 on our chart."

In much the same way, technical word charts can be developed as youngsters pursue major units in the content areas. Studying community helpers in first grade, youngsters talk about fire fighters and the equipment they use, such as ladders, nets, hoses, and fire engines. The teacher writes these words on the chart. When youngsters are ready to compose brief paragraphs about the equipment fire fighters use, they merely look up at their charts to find the words *ladders, nets, hoses,* and *fire engines* correctly spelled.

2. *Idea charting.* Teachers of young children also find that idea charting is a helpful device for beginning writers. On a large chart the teacher writes a key word or question important in their content-area study. For example, youngsters studying pets may focus on dogs. On top of one chart, the teacher may write "Words That Describe Dogs"; on top of another, "Things We Must Do to Care for Our Dog Pets"; on still another, "Why We Like Our Dog Pets." Children brainstorm all manner of words and ideas about dogs, which the teacher then records on the appropriate idea chart. Using the words and ideas on the chart that describes dogs, youngsters cooperatively write and revise sentences, which the teacher records for them on chart paper. Later, the youngsters can take the words and ideas from the second chart and compose individual paragraphs. The advantage of one idea on each chart is that the writing that results tends to focus on the one main idea. Thus the children begin to get a sense of paragraph structure.

3. *Framed paragraphs.* Giving youngsters a paragraph starter as a framework sometimes helps to get them writing, especially when they are working from a list of ideas and words on an idea chart. For example, youngsters drafting individual compositions from ideas on "Things We Must Do to Care for Our Pets" may benefit from a paragraph-starter such as:

We must take good care of our pets. We must _____

_____

and _____ .
Also we must _____

_____ .

In the blank spaces of the framed paragraph, students insert words from their charts.

4. *Repetitive paragraphs.* To help children who are just beginning to write independently, some teachers ask them to write paragraphs, each of which begin the same way. Thus on one day, children may talk and then write about times when they get angry. They begin their writing with "I get angry when . . ." On another day, children may talk about times when they are sad. That day their writing begins "I am sad when . . ." Through repetitive use, young writers soon master such basic words as *I, get, am* and *when.*

5. *Creative spelling.* As children begin to write independently, spelling poses a hurdle. Language arts specialists today more and more are advocating creative spelling, that is, letting children approximate the spelling of words, using their rudimentary sound-symbol system. When youngsters have talked about things in their immediate environment, they have much to write. To make them overly concerned about spelling is to cut off their stream of ideas when they write.

The strategies described above are part of the repertoire used by many experienced primary teachers who want to involve youngsters in creative composition. These same strategies can be used in content learning, for in the process of expressing ideas on paper, primary youngsters are learning concepts; they are learning through writing as well as learning to write.

Refining Writing Skills Beyond the Primary Grades

Once youngsters have gained some skill in writing, they are ready to refine these skills to produce good expository writing. To generate the ideas for writing, young people need opportunity:

1. To observe and record based on firsthand observations.
2. To translate data from visual to verbal forms.
3. To generalize based on their observations and on data read or heard.
4. To render judgments.
5. To apply generalizations to explain related situations.

At this point too, young people need guidance in handling data so they can write about relationships with clarity and precision. Let us consider next specific ways to involve upper grade students with both the content and craft of writing.

Brainstorming, Categorizing, and Generalizing. An instructional sequence that uses content for teaching writing has three components: brainstorming, categorizing, and generalizing through group writing.

1. *Brainstorming* is a useful technique for generating content for writing. Freely expressing any and all points that come to mind on a topic and listing these in the random order in which they surface is the essence of brainstorming. However, there must be an information base if brainstorming is to be used effectively. This means that the teacher who decides to use brainstorming as an instructional strategy leading to writing must provide students an opportunity to acquire a factual background. Accordingly, data gathering must precede brainstorming.

In a content unit on China, for example, data gathering can consist of reading or viewing a filmstrip, film, transparency, or picture series. It can consist of firsthand investigation or observation. Once participants have acquired some factual background, they gather together and in a freewheeling atmosphere call out information, ideas, and points of view. Several scribes record items on the board in the order given with no attempt to identify patterns or relationships.

2. *Categorizing.* Once ideas are recorded, the next step is to organize them into categories or around "big ideas." The teacher might begin, "This point seems to relate to agriculture in China. What other points also focus on this same subtopic?" As students identify related points, a scribe circles them with yellow chalk and a volunteer records each circled point on a chart. Working through the other points, the class cooperatively comes up with other categories such as Education in China, Industry in China, Government in China, Geography of China. In each category a scribe circles the points with a different colored chalk, and a volunteer lists related items on a chart.

3. *Generalizing in group writing.* Once all the points have been grouped into "big idea" categories, the teacher guides the students in thinking through possible relationships among the data. The class is now ready to compose cooperatively a paragraph that expresses these relationships along with supporting points. The teacher might begin by focusing on one category, for example, Agriculture in China; and ask, "Looking at all these points about the way agriculture is carried on in China, what can we say is generally true about farming methods there?" As students throw out ideas in this prewriting discussion, the teacher guides them in drafting a statement that becomes a topic sentence for a paragraph, which is then recorded on the board.

Students next identify points that back up the stated generalization. These become supporting sentences in the paragraph that gradually takes form on the board. Later, the teacher and students revise and edit the sentences they have drafted, giving attention to sentence order, sentence structure, word choice, and such mechanical matters as spelling, punctuation, capitalization, and usage.

Brainstorming, Categorizing, Judging. To get students thinking in the judgmental mode, a teacher would structure the instructional sequence somewhat differently. After students brainstorm and categorize, the teacher might ask, "Do you think that the agricultural system in China is better than that in the United States? Why? Do you think that the system in the United States is better than that in China? Why?" As the class offers opinions and makes judgments, two scribes record on the board. One lists points that support the position that the U.S. system is better than the Chinese; the other lists points that support the opposite position. During the discussion, the teacher may have to raise questions about the meaning of the word *better;* does it mean more productive? more democratic? more equitable?

Once the class has developed a list of points supporting each position, drafting short position paragraphs is a next step. If students have had some previous group-writing experience in drafting judgmental paragraphs, they can undertake this assignment in three-person writing teams. Each team selects a position (i.e., China's system is better; or the U.S. system is better). Later, teams that have taken different positions can merge to form six-person rewriting groups. Their task now is to write a short composition giving both the pros and cons. In this type of rewriting, teams may have to use transitional words (*however, on the other hand, yet, but, nevertheless, regardless*) to express relationships among the sentences.

Teachers who have used this sequence find that having teams record their paragraphs on the chalkboard or on large charting paper is helpful, because team members can see their first draft as they make suggestions for improving sentence and paragraph patterns.

Brainstorming, Categorizing, Outlining, and Drafting. In the two instructional sequences described above, the group's prewriting activities of brainstorming, categorizing, and talking about relationships occupies more time than the actual drafting of ideas into sentences and paragraphs. Some teachers who have used these approaches extend prewriting to include outlining of the points that have been categorized. Through outlining, students are identifying relationships they will later express in paragraph form.

A fifth-grade teacher, Janet Gould, did this for a unit on the People's Republic of China. Below is an outline developed by Ms. Gould's agriculture team, reproduced just as the team drafted it, so the reader will note some inconsistencies. However, the outline shows that these youngsters thought through and identified key relationships and developed an outline that will aid later in paragraph writing.

China's Agriculture

I. Products
    A. Rice is the most important resource
        1. South China produces
        2. Rice is raked by hand
    B. What is produced in North China
    C. Corn
    D. Soy beans
    E. Millet
    F. Fruit trees
II. Problems
    A. Shortage of land
    B. Food Supply is critical
    C. Machinery is scarce
    D. Buffaloes are used on farms
    E. Crops are harvested in traditional ways
III. Improvements being made
    A. Land is terraced so more can be used
    B. Dams are being built for irrigation
    C. Meetings are held to decide how the fields will be handled
    D. Farms are joined together to make a big farm called communes

Paragraph writing was the next step in Ms. Gould's unit on China. The team members who had made the outline on China's agricultural system each took one of the main headings and wrote a paragraph that included the given information. Later, they combined their paragraphs to form a short, informative piece on their topic.

Learning to Organize Longer Reports

Eventually students must learn to handle information gleaned from several sources and meld it into a series of paragraphs that flow logically one into another. Most teachers know that this is no easy task, even for adults. It requires the writer to identify major ideas on the topic and to organize data from more than one source into categories, which later become paragraphs in a written report.

One of the most useful tools for compiling data from a number of sources is the data retrieval chart. (See figure 12.)

Figure 12   DATA RETRIEVAL CHART ON COLONIAL AMERICA

Name of Researcher: _____ Subtopic Investigated: _____
I. Directions: Record in the appropriate column material on the the subtopic from the reference named. Each member of your three-person team will collect data from one of the references named and complete one column of the chart.

References	Middle Colonies	Southern Colonies	New England Colonies
textbook: *Your America*			
textbook:			
World Book			

II. Directions: When each member of your team has gathered data from one reference named, compile your data on one master chart. Then using the data from that chart, complete the following writing assignments:
   A. Draft a paragraph that describes schooling in the New England colonies.

   B. Draft a paragraph that describes schooling in the Middle colonies.

   C. Draft a paragraph that describes schooling in the Southern colonies.

   D. In your group, decide where you would have preferred to live during colonial days. Draft a paragraph expressing your preference based on the schooling practices there. Make sure your paragraph tells why.

In making a data retrieval chart, the first step is to identify the major topics to be investigated. Studying life in Colonial America, Ms. Donahue's fifth-grade class decided that a logical division was the New England Colonies, the Middle Colonies, and the Southern Colonies. Once they had these divisions in mind, they subdivided them according to cultural features in each colonial region (e.g., why the colony started, religion, housing, schooling, and farming practices).

For data-gathering purposes, Ms. Donahue divided her class into three-person teams. Each team focused on one of the subtopics identified (e.g., schooling, housing, etc.) and gathered information by reading in one of the references listed on the data retrieval chart. The students recorded their data in the appropriate category on the chart and later pooled their data so that each team member had information from several sources.

The next step was paragraph drafting. In the example cited above, each team member contributed sentences to paragraphs about life in each of the colonial regions using material directly from their retrieval charts. Here is the composition written by one team on colonial crops and trading goods.

Crops and Trading Goods in the Colonies

Some of the trade goods of New England were cloth, fish, and farm produce. They also built ships.

The middle colonies produced trade goods such as flax, hemp, cloth, corn, butter, cheese, and farming products. They became known as The "Bread basket." They also exported large quantities of pork and beef as well as crafts and furs to the West Indies.

The crop and trade goods of the Southern Colonies were tobacco, rice, pitch, tar, cattle, fish, lumber, blubber, whale oil, corn, wheat, and indigo. They traded sheepwool and things that they wove. On most plantations a new kind of tobacco was grown which sold for a lot in England.

As the young writers in the "school group" and in the "crops group" were gathering data and drafting paragraphs, others were working on different subtopics. When all groups had finished their paragraphs, the class compiled all the paragraphs into a major report with each section set off by topical headings.

Teachers using data retrieval charts for purposes of data gathering, data organizing, and paragraph drafting may wish at some point to help children go beyond the facts to generalize and render judgments. This, Ms. Donahue did with the writing assignment on the chart: "Decide where you would have preferred to live during colonial days. Draft a paragraph expressing your preference based on the schooling practices there. Make sure your paragraph tells why." This type of question asks students to render a judgment. The students orally shared their preference paragraphs and compared their points of view. Here, writing led to discussion rather than the other way around.

When students work cooperatively to produce a rather lengthy, composite report, the teacher can also help them think through major conclusions by involving them in a group writing of a final section that points out the relationships discovered. Here the teacher's job is to ask "Why? Why is it the way it is?" The students discuss the major relationships and then cooperatively draft a paragraph to conclude their report. In the example on Colonial America described in this section, the class composed this concluding paragraph that embodies a basic relationship that became evident from their previous reading, organizing, and writing activity:

The Early Colonies

As you can see, where the Colonies were located affected the kinds of houses the people lived in, the kind of schooling they had, and their crops and trading goods. With modern equipment we have found ways to overcome geographical limitations.

Thinking and Writing in a Variety of Modes

In upper elementary grades, as students grow in their ability to think abstractly, they need opportunity to think and write in a variety of modes. They need writing assignments that ask them to think about content from different perspectives. Such modes include asking students to:

1. Describe firsthand observations, tell how to do something, retell, and summarize;
2. Compare, contrast, analyze, and explain why;
3. Predict, guess, generalize, devise;
4. Express feelings and render opinions, preferences, and judgments;
5. Create stories.

A complete writing program in upper grades should include at some point opportunities to compose in all of these modes. For example, a series of assignments in seventh-grade science could include these specific assignments: describe what you saw happening during the experiment with magnesium; compare and contrast what happened when we burned magnesium to what happened when we burned paper and then wood; write a paragraph explaining why these materials burned differently; predict what will happen with an element such as sodium and give the reasons for your prediction; write a paragraph describing how you felt when you saw sodium burst into flames; create a story that has as a plot feature the rapid combustion of elements.

In the same way, older students can write paragraphs that vary structurally. They can write paragraphs that:

1. Begin with a topic sentence followed by supporting detail;
2. Begin with details that lead into a final topic sentence offering a generalization;
3. Compare and contrast two items;
4. Relate a series of events in chronological order.

Even in junior high and high school, teacher-guided group writing is a useful strategy for demonstrating different ways of structuring a paragraph to the class. Or the teacher can organize guided writing as a small-group activity with five or six students, while others pursue writing or reading tasks independently. After gaining experience through teacher-guided group writing, students can undertake a similar writing task on their own in other content areas.

Summary

This chapter has described ways of teaching writing as part of content learning, especially in science and social studies programs. These same approaches have application in art, music, and physical education. For example, youngsters who have seen and heard a clarinet and a trumpet can brainstorm words and ideas and then write paragraphs of description or reaction. In so doing, they gain writing power even as they come to a fuller understanding of the qualities of these musical instruments.

This chapter has also stressed report writing. This is not to say that poetry, stories, and other types of creative writing have no place in content-area studies. Clearly, young people can create haikus, acrostics, and diamantes as part of science; they can write lyrics to songs of their own creation in music classes; they can create original folktales patterned after ones representative of a culture they are studying.

Four major generalizations serve to summarize this chapter:
1. Writing in the content areas is not just a matter of making assignments. Writing requires considerable information gathering, prewriting, drafting, and rewriting if students are to master the skills of composition.
2. Teachers can make writing easier for students by providing them with such tools as data retrieval charts, categoized lists of brainstormed points, and idea and word charts.
3. Teaching writing skills is not necessarily an individual pursuit. Teacher-guided group writing and rewriting as well as small-team writing and rewriting are frameworks for teaching writing in the content areas.
4. Writing in the content areas cannot be divorced from reading, listening, and speaking. At the same time that children are involved in writing, they are gaining practice in other communication skills and they are learning essential content in unit studies.

Related References

Beyer, Barry, *et al.* "Writing to Learn in the Social Studies." *Social Education* 43 (March 1979). (This issue contains a number of articles on writing.)

Britton, James, *et al. The Development of Writing Abilities.* London: Macmillan Education, 1975.

Combs, Warren. "Further Effects of Sentence-Combining Practice on Writing Ability." *Research in the Teaching of English* 10 (Fall 1976): 137-149.

Crowhurst, Marion. "Developing Syntactic Skill: Doing What Comes Naturally." *Language Arts* 56 (May 1979): 522-525.

Donlan, D. "Music and the Language Arts Curriculum." *English Journal* 63 (October 1974): 86-88.

Graves, Donald. "An Examination of the Writing Processes of Seven Year Old Children." *Research in the Teaching of English* 9 (1975): 227-241.

_____. "Let's Get Rid of the Welfare Mess in the Teaching of Writing." *Language Arts* 53 (September 1976): 645-651.

Hamilton, David. "Writing Science." *College English* 40 (September 1978): 32-40.

Haynes, Elizabeth. "Using Research in Preparing to Teach Writing." *English Journal* 67 (January 1978): 82-88.

Hennings, Dorothy, and Grant, Barbara. *Written Expression in the Language Arts.* New York: Teachers College Press, 1981.

Lundsteen, Sara, ed. *Help for the Teacher of Written Compsition (K-9): New Directions in Research.* Urbana, Ill.: National Council of Teachers of English, 1976.

McKenzie, Gary. "Data Charts: A Crutch for Helping Pupils Organize Reports." *Language Arts* 56 (October 1979): 784-788.

Mellon, John. *Transformational Sentence-Combining: A Method for Enhancing the Development of Syntactic Fluency in English Composition.* Urbana, Ill.: National Council of Teachers of English, 1969.

Moffett, James. "Integrity in the Teaching of Writing." *Phi Delta Kappan* 61 (December 1979): 276-279.

National Assessment of Educational Progress. *Write/Rewrite: An Assessment of Revision Skills.* Denver, Colo.: National Assessment of Educational Progress, 1977.

_____ . *Writing Mechanics, 1969-1974: A Capsule Description of Changes in Writing Mechanics.* Denver, Colo.: National Assessment of Educational Progress, 1975.

O'Hare, Frank. *Sentence-Combining: Improving Student Writing Without Formal Grammar Instruction.* Urbana, Ill.: National Council of Teachers of English, 1973.

Perron, Jack. *The Impact of Mode on Written Syntactic Complexity, Parts I, II, and III.* Eric Documents # 126 531 and #125 511.

_____ . "Beginning Writing: It's All in the Mind." *Language Arts* 53 (September 1976): 652-57.

Press, Harriet Baylor. "Basic Motivation for Basic Skills: The Interdependent Approach to Interdisciplinary Writing." *College English* 41 (November 1979): 310-313.

Sealey, Leonard, *et al. Children's Writing: An Approach for the Primary Grades.* Newark, Del.: International Reading Association, 1979.

Sisk, Dorothy. "Integrating the Arts with Language Arts." *Gifted Child Quarterly* 20 (Winter 1976): 497-500.

Todd, Lewis. "Writing," in *Skill Development in the Social Studies, 33rd Yearbook of the National Council for the Social Studies.* Washington, D.C.: National Council for the Social Studies, 1963.

Conclusions

In most elementary schools the teacher is responsible for instruction in social studies and current events, in general science and mathematics, in health and physical education, and in art, music, and literature, while at the same time teaching children to read and write, to listen and speak, and to use language to think. In handling these curriculum components, too often the teacher perceives them as discrete and distinctive parts without realizing that the teaching of communication and reading skills cannot be separated from the teaching of content. Communicating and reading are processes that students can master best through handling content. This content can be stories and poems—our literary heritage; it can be current events, science, social studies, health, art, and music. All content areas should be utilized if students are to develop their communication and reading skills to the fullest. For this most basic of reasons, the elementary teacher must blend the teaching of language skills with the teaching of content.

Upper grade and secondary school teachers find the task of blending skills and content more difficult, because they usually have responsibility for only one content area and think of themselves as teachers of science, social studies, or music. With limited time for teaching their specialties, secondary teachers fear that attention given to language skills development will infringe on content learning. Such fears are unfounded. As *Teaching Communication and Reading Skills in the Content Areas* has emphasized, listening, speaking, reading, and writing are ways of learning content. As students write, they are thinking through content and coming to a better understanding of it. As students learn to read and listen, they are learning how to learn content. As students build vocabulary, they are gaining a better grasp on the technical terminology that is an inherent part of a discipline. Accordingly, instruction in the content areas is often the most productive place for teaching reading and communication skills. Young people are acquiring skills even as they use those skills to learn.